All proceeds from the sale of this book will be designated for the General and Mrs. Seth J. McKee, USAF (Ret.) Scholarship at the Southeast Missouri University Foundation. This scholarship has been established to support students attending Southeast Missouri State University who have served or are currently serving in the United States military.

For ordering, email Foundation@semo.edu.

ISBN: 978-0-578-73988-5 (Paperback)
ISBN: 978-0-578-73987-8 (Hardcover)

Printed by Sheridan Books, Inc.

First printing edition 2020

Kellerman Foundation for Historic Preservation
102 Main St
Cape Girardeau, MO 63701

www.kellermanfoundation.org

KELLERMAN FOUNDATION
FOR HISTORIC PRESERVATION

Seth★ ★ ★ ★

THE LIFE AND JOURNEY OF GENERAL SETH JEFFERSON MCKEE

Best Wishes

Jay Ford

Frank Mitchell

To Sally

Table of Contents

Acknowledgments.. xiv

Introduction... xvii

PART 1
Memories

Young Life 2

Farming...13

One-Room Schoolhouse 26

High School 35

College 43

National Guard...50

Westward Ho...56

Wrestling..73

Army Air Corps..82

PART 2
Military Service

Fighter Pilot 88

Statesman 98

USS *Pueblo*...103

Photos

The Early Years...109

WWII 111

NORAD 117

Presidents, Awards 127

The McKees 133

PART 2
(Continued)

NORAD 143
Six Presidents..146
Reflections..149
Military Awards and Decorations 154
The General Seth J. McKee Award.......................157

PART 3
The Amazing McKees

Family Time 160
Visiting Home 173
Retirement Years..178
"Pop"..182
Tributes To Sally Parshall McKee 185

Appendix...190
Index 204

"Regardless of the level of responsibility that you hold as you travel through life, if you make every effort to be the best among your peers at that level, your superiors will take notice and appropriately move you up the ladder to the next higher level on an accelerated schedule. If you have the capability to do that at every level you achieve in life, you will eventually end up among those at the top."

– General Seth J. McKee

General Seth J. McKee

1916-2016

ACKNOWLEDGMENTS

This book is divided into three sections. The first section, entitled "Memories," is primarily an autobiography by General McKee, and provides glimpses of his young years. Dr. Frank Nickell, retired historian at Southeast Missouri State University, and I independently organized McKee's text into paragraphs and chapters. We reviewed our notes and agreed on the few differences. Then it was a matter of correcting spelling, punctuation, grammar and submitting to our editor Mickey Heath, at Southeast Missouri State University's Center for Writing Excellence, for the finishing touches.

The other two sections, "Military Service" and "The Amazing McKees," were more difficult and took substantial time to complete. They were like solving giant jigsaw puzzles. It took a village. The McKee family shared valuable information. We compiled General McKee's recollections throughout his years as told to his family and friends. Additional information was gleaned from newspaper accounts of his exploits, personal interviews, family scrapbooks, military records, citations, awards, the archives of the *Southeast Missourian* newspaper in Cape Girardeau, Missouri, and several newspapers in Japan, as well as Southeast Missouri State University archives and personal interviews with myself and Dr. Nickell.

The interviews with McKee were, by nature, similar. His mind was always alert and time and again he would remember more facts, figures, personalities, stories, and events over the decades with remarkable clarity. Key components remained the same and vivid in his mind as if they occurred yesterday.

Thank you to the entire McKee family, the general's amazing lifelong partner, Sally, and their three sons Jeff, Bill, and Tom. It doesn't take long for one to appreciate their intellect, patriotism, and accomplishments. They always made time for me regardless of their personal schedules. They gave critical background and insight to many of Seth's recollections. I will always be grateful for their support and cooperation for this project. Locally in Cape Girardeau, sisters-in-law Jodie and Peggy McKee, nieces Tami Holshouser and Cheri Landgraf, nephews Brad McKee and Luke Landgraf, and other family members provided their personal recollections, sometimes with unique embellishments. We had fun reminiscing about old times sitting around their various kitchen tables.

My wife, Margaret, provided initial editorial comment in the early days and months of this project and continued her considerable patience, as she has in all my other projects. Jay Eastlick, formerly with the *Southeast Missourian* and the newspaper, provided additional information in their columns from interviews with General McKee. Thanks also to our printer, Sheridan Publishing, and their representative, Jessica Ansorge, for her guidance in organizing information into a cohesive unit. She helped solve the puzzle. Special mention goes to my stepson-in-law Scott Lorenz and Justin White from The Wright Group in Cape Girardeau for providing tutoring assistance to this word processor novice throughout the process and helping with selection and saving of photos. Scott also designed the front cover and various other items throughout the book. Dr. Nickell's niece, Sara Stewart, also provided assistance with some of the photos. The final piece of the puzzle came together when Cassi Daugette's placement of photos, maps, charts, and other materials into the body of the text provided icing on the cake. She also finished the Index—no small feat.

And to my cohort, Dr. Frank Nickell, who kept me grounded as we traveled this journey together. His years of authoring, editing, publishing, tutoring, and extensive contacts within the literary community throughout our region are legendary. Frank, I can't thank you enough. Also, a shout-out goes to the memory of Dick Kent Withers, who assisted Dr. Nickell for several years chronicling McKee and other subjects of history in and around Cape Girardeau with his trusty video camera, and a lifetime personal friend of mine. He is missed.

Jerry Ford

INTRODUCTION

Men have looked to the skies and pondered flight for centuries. The Wright Brothers spent the first ten years of the 20th Century perfecting their flying machines. 1903 is the year attributed to their first real flight of consequence. With that short flight, aviation was born. A few years later, a boy was born in rural Arkansas who also became fascinated with flight and would spend his entire life as a pilot.

SETH JEFFERSON MCKEE was born in McGehee, Arkansas, in 1916, and spent most of his childhood in Cape Girardeau, Missouri. He rose from a rural farm boy to become one of America's most highly decorated members of the United States Air Force.

McKee was an active participant in the liberation of Europe in WWII, Commander of US Forces Japan and 5th Air Force during Vietnam, on the front lines of the Cold War, and Commander-in-Chief of NORAD. At the time of his death at the age of 100 in December of 2016, he was the oldest four-star general in our nation as well as the highest-ranking survivor of the

D-Day Invasion, where he led a group of fighter planes providing air cover for the troops on the beaches of Normandy in 1944.

During those years he flew his P-38 Lightning fighter-bomber (My Gal Sal) in Northern France, Germany, Ardennes-Alsace, and central Europe, logging 190 hours of flying time in 69 combat missions. He was promoted to Brigadier General at age 42, the youngest Air Force officer to be named a star rank.

Along the way McKee also held command and operations positions in France, Belgium and Germany. His many positions included deputy commander and later commander 370th Fighter Group, England; 12th Air Force March Air Force Base, California; chief technical advisor to the Italian Air Force Rome, Italy; commander 36th Fighter Bomber Group, Europe; commander 2nd Bombardment Wing Hunter Air Force Base, Georgia; commander 823rd Air Division Homestead Air Force Base, Florida; director of plans Strategic Air Command Offutt Air Force Base, Nebraska; commander 821st Strategic Aerospace Division Ellsworth Air Force Base, South Dakota; assistant chief of staff plans and operations U.S. Headquarters, Washington, DC, for Joint Chief of Staff matters; commander US Forces, Japan and 5th Air Force Fuchu Air Station, Japan; assistant vice chief of staff, U.S. Air Force, Washington, D.C.; and commander-in-chief NORAD/CONAD/ADC Ent Air Force Base, Colorado.

Years later, television personality Tom Brokaw penned the men and women of WWII as *The Greatest Generation.* Interview after interview revealed most who served never talked about their experiences to their family, friends, or the public. They didn't consider themselves heroes or special. When asked, McKee would answer, "I was just doing my job."

While General McKee was one of our nation's most resolute decorated warriors, he abhorred war. He was quoted as saying, "When man has to resort to war to resolve his affairs, he's reached about his lowest level. We're back to the cave-man days where you grab a club."

The genesis for this book began five years ago (2015) when my lifelong friend, Dewey Schade, invited me to attend the grand opening of The Nash, a new jazz club in Phoenix, Arizona, named for Lewis Nash, a great jazz drummer originally from Phoenix. The event featured the great jazz trumpeter, Wynton Marsalis. Being a fairly accomplished jazz trumpet player myself, I couldn't resist. During those three exhilarating days, I arranged for Dewey to have lunch with me and retired General McKee, a resident of Scottsdale, Arizona, who had grown up in our hometown of Cape Girardeau, Missouri. The Ford and McKee families have been lifelong friends.

We began what was to be a short lunch but turned into an afternoon dissertation by General McKee on four wars, seven presidents, D-Day, Japan, the USS *Pueblo* Incident, NORAD and much more, *and me without a tape recorder.* It was four of the most historically enlightening hours of my life.

Upon return to Cape Girardeau, I happened to encounter Dr. Frank Nickell, a retired history professor at our local college, Southeast Missouri State University. He was completing four years as regional director of the State Historical Society of Missouri and had completed an oral interview of General McKee. I informed him of my recent lunch with the general and he said as far as he knew, "Seth McKee was probably the only USAF four-star general that did not have a book written about him." I immediately responded, "Well, let's do it!"

So here we are in 2020. It's been quite a ride. Learn, appreciate, and enjoy the life of an American icon, General Seth J. McKee.

PART 1
MEMORIES

"I learned hard work and moral ethics on the farm.
Cultivating 25 acres with one plow and a pair of mules for
several weeks taught you to finish the job."

– General Seth J. McKee

YOUNG LIFE

Early on the morning of 6 November 1916, I have been led to believe I vocally announced my arrival in McGehee, Arkansas, USA, with a volume that probably awakened everyone within a block of our home. In those days, practically all baby deliveries were made at home, as was I. Although I soon recognized and became quite fond of the wonderful lady that nursed and cared for me, it was some time before I was aware that she was my mother and that I was the son of William Ferdinand McKee and Jeffie Olivia Warrington McKee and that I had a sister named Angie Arneita who had arrived approximately two years before I did. "Neit" and I bonded early.

To the best of my knowledge, my father was born 15 September 1890, in Jefferson County, Missouri. He was raised on a farm and attended school under the tutelage of his father in a one-room school house that accommodated the first through eighth grades. He quit school at an early age and I presume he farmed until he left home and found work on the railroad. In a short time, he became an engineer and first sighted my mother from his engine cab while passing her father's plantation located near McGehee, Arkansas. After several such sightings, during which they started waving to each other, he made a visit to McGehee, discovered who she was and made a call at her foster parents' home. This eventually led to a wedding in 1913.

My mother was a sweet, gentle person who was raised on a plantation by her aunt and her uncle after her mother's death while giving birth to her. She was born in early 1895, and while growing up, was educated in the local grammar school and high school. She was a beautiful "Southern Belle," and it is easy to understand why my father became so infatuated with her. She was a key figure in my life and that of my brothers and sisters. Although she passed away many years ago, she will always serve as a role model for all that knew her. In the early 1970s, she was selected as runner-up mother of the year in the State of Missouri. In the opinion of her children and others who knew her well, she should have been designated mother of the year or century.

My father being a railway engineer necessitated that our family move frequently during the first 10 years or so of my life. It was always a move from one small town in Arkansas or southeast Missouri to another as the Cotton Belt or Frisco railroad needs dictated. New siblings arrived at approximately two-year intervals until I had a total of three brothers and three sisters, making a total of seven children in the family. We were, in order of arrival, Neit, as previously mentioned, myself, Edward A. (better known as Pete), Willa Dee (Dee), Glen, William F. (Pat), and Olivia (Ebbie). An eighth child, Albert Lee (Al), joined us 10 years later, but I had left the family home prior to his arrival. There were no introverts among us, and I have many happy memories of escapades involving one or more of us during our early years.

I was named after my grandfathers, Seth G. McKee and

Jefferson Warrington. Grandpa McKee was born in Jefferson County, Missouri, in 1862 and lived to be 94 years of age. In his younger years, he was a schoolteacher in Carter County, Missouri, and in later years worked on the railroad and served as chief of police in De Soto, Missouri. Grandma McKee died when I was around 4 years old, and one of my early memories is of an ambulance picking her up at our home while she was visiting us at Kennett, Missouri. Unfortunately, she had a ruptured appendix and did not survive, as there were no antibiotics in those days to combat the resulting infection. Fortunately, she did get to see her son and four daughters grow up and see five of her grandchildren before her death at 59 years of age.

Grandpa McKee lived for another 38 years and was a very important figure in our family until his death. I have limited knowledge of Grandpa and Grandma Warrington, my mother's parents. Grandma Warrington died giving birth to my mother and Grandpa Warrington, being much older than his deceased wife, entrusted my mother's rearing to his sister and her husband, Papa Burch. Grandpa Warrington owned a large cotton plantation in southeast Arkansas which his family had owned and operated since long before the Civil War. He was a fully grown man before that war, but I have no idea what role, if any, he played during the war. Since his plantation bordered the Mississippi River, his plantation did receive cannon fire from Union rivercraft on occasion, according to my mother.

In 1919 or 1920, we moved from Missouri to McNeil, Arkansas, and remained there for approximately two years. It was from 1919 or so that my memory of events begins and is thus revealed herein. McNeil was, and I presume still is, a small railroad town between Little Rock and Texarkana where all homes were within three or four blocks of the railroad yards and the main line tracks. I still remember the troop trains passing through and my waving to the soldiers on their way home from

World War I. I also remember the time that I, at age 5, in company with my brother Pete (age 3), decided to take a closer look at trains in the switching yards, although we were forbidden to go near them. Since we only lived a couple of blocks from the rail yards we managed to slip out of our yard at home without our mother or older sister catching us in the act and managed to reach the rail yards with no difficulty. Fortunately, we found several freight trains in the yards in a stationary position, and it didn't take us long to decide that we should take a closer look.

The caboose of the nearest train wasn't very far from us, so I boosted Pete up on the first step (it was too high for him to manage) and then climbed up behind him. The door on the rear platform was open, so we entered to take a look at the crew accommodations and whatever else was contained therein. Fortunately, there were no train crew members there, but unfortunately, before we had time to complete our inspection, we felt the train start to move.

It hadn't occurred to me that this might happen, but I immediately understood that if we didn't disembark immediately, serious consequences would result. Since it was a long freight train it took some time to get underway but by the time we got to the rear platform it was probably moving at the rate of three or 4 miles per hour. Of course, we had no option but to get on the lowest step as soon as possible and then jump, which we did. As the bottom step was some two feet or so above the roadbed and the train was probably moving at a speed of 5 miles an hour, Pete and I immediately became a couple of tumbling balls alongside the railroad track. Fortunately, no more scratches or bruises were acquired than in our normal activities, so our parents didn't learn of our escapade until many years later.

I have many other memories of living in McNeil. One is Pete's attempt to teach baby chickens to swim like baby ducks in a rain barrel. (They never learned.) Another is playing with the little black boy of my age every week when he accompanied his mother to our house where she would do the weekly laundry. He taught me how to fill our corrals we built of dirt with "livestock" we collected from the vegetable garden. I, of course, knew they were really potato bugs. I got my first flight training by launching my little red wagon, with some makeshift wings attached, from the roof of a small storage building in our backyard. That didn't work very well, either. I saw my first movie, a silent picture starring Charlie Chaplin, with a canvas tent as the theater, and many, many other firsts in my young life were experienced there.

It was also in McNeil I first enrolled in public schools. In those days there were no preschools or kindergartens where we lived, so in September 1922 my sister Neit and I enrolled in the first grade of the local school. Also, in those days there were no school buses, so we walked the few blocks involved, as did all other students. Neit and I ended up in the same grade from the first through the 12th due to the fact my birthday is in November. So I was permitted to enroll while I was still 5 years old. Neit, whose birthday was in February, could not enroll until she was over 6½ years old. Additionally, she missed enrolling the next year due to illness (typhoid), thereby making us classmates for the first 12 years of our schooling, a circumstance that pleased both of us. I only attended school in McNeil for one year and don't remember too much about school there, but I must have done okay, as I have among my memorabilia a highly complimentary report from my teacher attesting my performance.

In 1923 we moved to Springdale, Arkansas, and remained there, or in the vicinity, for three years. We lived in three different places during our sojourn there, the first of which was in a large house located on a couple of acres that included a vegetable garden and a barn. The property was located at the edge of town on the highway that led to Fayetteville, which was only a

6

few miles away. This was a gravel road (as were most highways in the Midwest in those days with the exception of those on the outskirts of major cities) and the great majority of the traffic was horse-drawn. Actually, there were many highways in Arkansas and Missouri yet to be graveled.

My memories of this period of my life are many and varied. I remember it was in the second and third grades here that I became so interested in reading, a pastime I still enjoy. Even during summer months when school was not in session, I spent my time reading children's adventure stories including the "Bobbsey Twins" and all others of this ilk I could find in the local library.

As the oldest boy in the family, it was largely my responsibility to attend to the vegetable garden, and many were the times that my mother found me in the shade reading a book when I was supposed to be weeding the garden or attending to other tasks. Fortunately, my mother was very understanding and actually encouraged me in my reading, except for those times it interfered with more immediate responsibilities.

Other memories include catching a runaway milk cow I then tied to a tree on our front lawn. It wasn't long until her owner came by looking for her and gave me one dollar for my actions. That was the most money I remember having up until that time, so I made it a point to keep my eyes open for runaway animals for the rest of that summer.

A little later that summer, strawberry picking time arrived and I found employment as a strawberry picker at one of the many strawberry farms on the outskirts of Springdale. Strawberry pickers were paid according to the number of boxes of berries they picked. I don't recall how many boxes I picked that year, but I do recall I picked enough to earn 25 or 30 dollars. Never having had that much money before (as a child I never received a monetary allowance), I entrusted my earnings to my mother, who suggested I discuss what I should do with it with my father when he returned home from railroad duty in another part of the state.

When my father returned, he advised I should buy a horse saddle. Since we didn't own a horse, I had some difficulty understanding my need for a saddle, but my father assured me that every boy should own a saddle. I guess my father, having grown up in the days of the horse and buggy, didn't fully understand that those days were rapidly coming to an end. However, being 8 years of age at the time, I believed his judgment to be infallible. I soon found myself the proud possessor of a beautifully tooled leather horse saddle. I will admit that I did use it once about five years later when we lived on a farm in Missouri and I saddled old "Sam," a mule I was well acquainted with, and rode him to church one Sunday. I don't recall using it any other time, but I think my father got some use out of it in the early 1940s when he purchased a Tennessee Walking Horse.

By then I had been gone from home for a few years and using a parachute to sit on in lieu of a saddle. Shortly after I bought the saddle, we moved to a farm some 15 miles from Springdale and lived there for a year or so. It was there my father purchased a pair of young mules (Pete and Sam), as he evidently decided that with three sons (later there were five) he would eventually be able to farm and still work as a railway engineer.

That was a fun time for me, as I was too small to handle the heavy machinery associated with farming, while the beautiful mountains and small streams offered endless adventure to an 8-year-old boy. The one-room schoolhouse we attended was just across a small stream about 200 yards from our front door. In addition to Pete and Sam, we had two or three milk cows, turkeys, and geese that would chase me, and chickens that I could chase. It was in the yard of this home, at about 4 or 5 o'clock one morning, that I saw the man in the moon. I don't know what keyed such a memorable event, but I still remember seeing every detail of that smiling face. My mother usually read to us every night for an hour or so by kerosene lamplight, so most likely something she had read had stirred my imagination.

During the times my father was away on railroad business, it was my responsibility to feed Pete and Sam, who were confined to a barn and a small barnyard. It was also my responsibility to lead them once a day to water, which welled from a spring into a large pool located about a quarter of a mile from the barn and was accessed via a path through the woods. Pete and Sam were only 3 years old and sometimes became quite frisky. I always led both of them to water at the same time by short halter ropes, and when one would rear up on his hind legs, the other would too. I quite often would find myself dangling in the air, about 4 feet off the ground, with a rope in each hand that I was afraid to let go of because I knew that I would have a very difficult time trying to catch the one that got loose. Fortunately, the path was rather narrow and confined by trees and brush so they were unable to rear in opposite directions. I also believe they knew that I was their benefactor and was young too, as they always permitted my very light weight to bring their front feet back to earth without too much fuss.

Another responsibility I had during my father's absence was to chop old wooden fence rails into the proper length to fit in the wood-burning stoves that were used to cook our food and to heat our home in the winter. Practically all fencing of animal pastures and cultivated fields in the area at that time consisted of wooden rails that had been in place since the earliest settlements. They were just beginning to be replaced by wire fencing, so there was an almost endless supply of old wooden rails available. I spent many hours slowly hacking my way through those rails, particularly in the wintertime. I used a double-bitted axe (with cutting blades on both sides) and managed to split my scalp once by swinging too far back on my backswing. Now, some 85 plus years later, I still have a large scar on the top of my head.

Fortunately, we had a good neighbor who would relieve me at the chopping block most times when he was passing our house and I was chopping wood. He could completely sever a length of wood from a rail with one swing. It required about 20 swings from me. Consequently, he could complete that daily chore for me in about five or 10 minutes.

During our early years, my mother always required that all of us children attend Sunday school on a regular basis. Although I remember Sunday school during the time we lived in Springdale, it was the small country church that we attended during the time that we lived on the farm that provided more lasting memories.

As was the custom at those small churches, most of the members vied for the honor of having the minister accompany them home for dinner (lunch) following services, which ended at 12 o'clock noon. My parents were frequently successful in this competition, and I was always happy when they were, as that meant we were going to have chicken and dumplings or fried chicken, both of which were my favorites. I guess that our minister was single, as he always came alone. The only problem was that the preacher always got my favorite piece of chicken, which was, as Mom carved a chicken, the pulley bone with most of both breasts still attached. In later years, when I visited home, Mom always spoiled me by ensuring that I received that choice piece.

I also recall the lengthy blessings the pastor provided for our meals. I might note here our entire family always sat down together for our meals three times a day, and every meal was preceded by a blessing from my mother. That custom has carried on down through the years in the families of all of her descendants, with most of them adopting her words. It was also during this time that "Jesus Loves Me" and "In the Garden" became my favorite songs and I sang or hummed them most of the time I was alone.

This was several years before the days that radios became the main source of our musical knowledge. We also learned songs at school, as all school days were started off by the teacher leading us in a few songs in the songbooks most country schools provided. Many of the songs were of pre-Civil War vintage and would be considered politically incorrect today. Some of them were beautiful songs, and fortunately, many of them have had enough word changes to make them acceptable today. Equally fortunate, none of them contained the gutter language that is heard in so many of today's so-called songs that we hear daily on radio and television programs. Of course, we did have phonographs, and I still remember the turntable with the big horn that sat on our living room table.

☆☆☆☆

The automobiles of the early twenties had no batteries or starters, so they had to be cranked by hand and many an arm was broken by the backfires that frequently occurred in the process. After the engine was running, electrical power for the spark plugs, lights, etc. was provided by the magneto. At night the headlights barely glowed at idle but brightened up as you increased engine speed. Fortunately, Charles Kettering (who later became a friend of mine) solved the broken arm problem by inventing the self-starter, which required a battery, thereby solving many other electrical problems in later years. I also recall Fords didn't have fuel gauges, and the amount of fuel in the tank had to be ascertained by removing the front seat to get to the tank and then measuring the fuel with a wooden stick that was calibrated in gallons for that purpose. This inconvenience led many Ford owners to be lax in keeping track of fuel on board, which in turn led to many stalled engines on roads up mountainsides. The Fords had no fuel pumps, so the engines were gravity fed from the fuel tank by a hole in the bottom front of the tank.

On uphill roads, of course, the fuel ran to the back of the tank, thereby uncovering the feed line and stalling the engine. The solution was to back up the steep slopes, which put the fuel tank above the engine and also made the fuel run to the front of the tank. It was not uncommon when driving uphill on a country road to pass one or more vehicles backing up the hill.

After an all-too-short stay in the scenic country near Springdale, we moved back to town and I resumed my schooling in the local elementary school, which seemed very large to me after my experience in the one-room country schoolhouse. The Springdale school was a two-story brick building with a separate room for each of its eight grades, and our total enrollment was in the hundreds. These numbers ensured much excitement in play and scrapping during recess and after school. Other than the arrival of my youngest sister Ebbie and my shooting of Pete in his posterior with my new air rifle when he was a little slow in jumping behind a tree, I don't recall too much happening that was other than routine in a family as large as ours during this period. Our father was away railroading most of the time, and Mom was keeping us children healthy and happy. However, this was all about to change.

FARMING

It was either late in l926 or early 1927 that my father announced that we were moving back to Missouri. I can only assume that railroading conditions dictated he look for additional means of supporting our family, and farming was his only option. I knew he had purchased a farm, sight unseen, in the Ozarks of southern Missouri that turned out to be an undeveloped mountaintop not accessible by road, so it wasn't clear to me where we were going to farm.

That point was cleared up when arrangements were made to move to Gordonville, Missouri, a very small town a few miles west of Cape Girardeau, Missouri, where my paternal grandfather and my father's four married sisters resided. That was good news, as we had visited my father's family in Cape on previous occasions and always had a great time with our loving aunts and a couple of cousins who were the ages of Neit and my brother Pete. Also, the husband of Aunt Nellie worked for the Coca-Cola Company, and there was never a shortage of "soda pop" of all flavors at their house.

The knowledge that the extended family routinely gathered at one of the families' homes on weekends and holidays for picnicking and visiting added to my anticipation. I recalled one visit we had made in the past when my cousin Delphine had let me ride her bicycle. I never owned a bike and had never ridden one before, but I had no problem. So, after a few minutes of riding, I decided I would like to venture further afield. To justify straying from the local area I made the magnanimous decision to buy an ice cream cone for all present with a dollar that I had earned picking berries. With that idea in mind, and without notifying anyone of my intentions, I peddled to a drugstore that was about six blocks away and announced to the "soda jerk" that I wanted to purchase 16 ice cream cones. (They only cost 5 cents each in those days.)

The clerk involved was happy to accommodate me, but first inquired how I planned to transport them. I, of course, proudly advised him I would use my bicycle, which had a basket attached to the handlebars. He, of course, advised me that all cones would have to be transported in an upright position or the ice cream would fall from the cone in the 90° temperature that existed at the time. After some thought the clerk went to the storeroom and returned with a piece of cardboard that measured about 12×20 inches, which he handed to me along with a pair of scissors. He then suggested that I cut 16 holes—equally spaced and about the size of a half dollar—in the cardboard, which I immediately proceeded to do.

That being done, he then carefully filled 16 cones with one large scoop of vanilla ice cream each, handing them to me one by one as he did so. Having carefully secured the cardboard in the basket of the bicycle (which he had permitted me to wheel into the store), I then placed each cone in one of the holes as securely as I could. After I had loaded the 16th cone, although the earlier loaded cones had started to melt, we both agreed that we had solved the problem of transportation well. While the clerk held the door open for me, I pushed the bike to the street with all the dignity and skill that an 8- or 9-year-old could muster, and proudly straddled my machine.

That wasn't too difficult, as it was a girl's bike and didn't have the same bars as boys' bikes do. With my left foot firmly on the pedal, I shoved off with my right foot in what I thought was a professional manner and although I wobbled a little I thought I had made a departure that most likely impressed anyone who might have been watching me. As soon as I felt I was in full control I looked at my ice cream cones and realized their speed of melting was greatly enhanced by the bright sunlight and I shouldn't tarry. With that thought in mind, I stood up on the pedals and started to pump as hard as I could.

About that time, a car pulled up to about 10 feet behind and with a blast of horn and squealing tires pulled around me. My reaction to this was to instinctively turn my wheel to the right as far and as fast as I could. This, of course, launched me over the handlebars onto the street while the bike and its load of ice cream cones slid down the street on its side right behind me. I quickly found that, with the exception of skinned knees and elbows, I was undamaged, so I then turned my attention to the ice cream and the bike, in that order. To my delight, I found that about half of the cones were still in the cardboard holder and the remainder were still in the basket or in the street quite near it where the bike was lying on its side.

I put the bike upright on its stand and discovered there appeared to be no damage done there. As rapidly as I could, I recovered my ice cream and after resetting each scoop in its respective cone I carefully replaced it in the holder with the cones that hadn't fallen out. I did note that they had melted down to about half size by then so I was quite confident that any germs that might have been picked up from the street had been washed away by the melt.

I safely made my way back to the family gathering and

proudly passed out a cone to everyone there. I made sure that the one I saved for myself was one that hadn't fallen from the cardboard container. I made no mention of my accident and other than commenting on how rapidly ice cream melted in 90-degree temperatures and commenting on what a big boy I was getting to be, little was said. So, with happy memories of Missouri as above, and anticipation of many more to come, I was certainly looking forward to our move.

Grandpa Seth Green McKee arrived in Springdale shortly before our scheduled date of departure and I learned that he was to accompany our furniture and livestock (two mules and a couple of milk cows), which would be shipped by the railroad. His job was to ensure that the livestock was properly watered and fed during the trip. He accomplished this by riding in the boxcar that contained our belongings, including the animals. I don't believe long-distance moving vans existed at that time, as our national highway system consisted primarily of dirt or gravel roads with some paving in the larger cities. That certainly was the case in the central states, and most everything was moved by rail.

Our family, which at that time consisted of Mom and Dad and seven children, varying in age from a couple of months to 12 years or so, all made the trip in a four-door Model T Ford. I don't recall too much about the trip of approximately 400 miles through the heart of the Ozarks, which must have taken at least two or three days over the dirt and gravel roads that then existed, but I do recall some of the fantastic scenery of the mountains we encountered. Other than a few flat tires due to puncture on the rough roads, which we repaired by patching the inner tubes with the repair kits that all cars carried, I don't remember any problems.

As I enjoyed these new adventures, it seemed only too

soon we arrived at our destination. We moved directly into a house we had rented in advance of our arrival in Gordonville. Gordonville only had a population of a couple of hundred or so, but it was the site of a consolidated school that had recently been constructed to serve the surrounding rural communities. Missouri was in the early stages of consolidating their country one-room schoolhouses in order to improve the quality of their educational system for rural children. After a one-year enrollment at this school, I was to experience three years of schooling at one-room schoolhouses, and there is considerable doubt in my mind that consolidated schools were necessarily better. Of the teachers I had in my elementary school years, the ones I remember best were from my three years in one-room schools.

I consider one of them among my best teachers from first grade through college. During our stay in Gordonville, I was in the fifth grade, and in addition to learning how to ice-skate, I was introduced to ciphering. For those who do not understand what ciphering is (as I didn't at the time), ciphering as it was practiced in the school at Gordonville was a mathematics contest pitting one half of the class against the other half. The teacher would name two team captains who would then take turns selecting other members of our class to be on their team. The teams would then line up in single file facing the blackboard. The teacher would then pose a problem of addition, subtraction, multiplication or division, and at the word *go* the first in line for each team would attempt to solve the problem before the other did. The loser of that contest would take his seat and the next boy or girl in line would take his or her place, and another problem would be presented for them to solve. This process would continue until all members of one of the teams had been defeated. This contest occurred most every Friday afternoon in the last hour before school let out for the weekend.

I found this great fun as, with all due modesty, I excelled in math in my grammar school years and it wasn't long before the teacher and I became the two captains to choose up sides every Friday afternoon. I found it to be even more fun when it turned out that I could solve the problems faster than the teacher, so my side usually won.

The ice-skating skills I acquired that winter were not nearly as impressive as my math skills. With a pair of clamp-on skates and use of a very small stream that was near Gordonville, which froze over most of that winter, I did acquire a limited ability to stand up on skates, which I further enhanced during my high school and college years in Cape Girardeau. I only recall being on skates one more time after my school years (in Garmisch, Germany) before I was called upon many years later to be the honorary referee at an international hockey match at the Broadmoor Hotel skating center in Colorado Springs, Colorado. Although it seemed that I was seldom skating on the blades of my skates, I did manage to remain on my feet during most of that occasion.

Our stay in Gordonville was relatively short, as in early spring the farm my father had been waiting for became available, and it was time to move on. Since the farm was only 10 miles or so west of Gordonville, moving consisted of loading the wagon with furniture and other assorted items and heading west. Of course, it took more than this one trip to move the furniture but I do not remember how many more were required. I do remember that on the first trip we also moved the two milk cows, which necessitated that my brother Pete and I make the trip on foot in order to drive the cows along behind the wagon, which was driven by my father. Although the trip seemed rather long, it was uneventful except during the time it took us to pass a neighboring farm, which was home to a bull who evidenced great interest in the two cows we were driving past. I was positive that he was going to jump the fence, so I spent a rather nervous half hour or so making sure I had an escape route available at all times. Fortunately, the fence served its purpose, and we got by unscathed.

The farm we were moving to was located on Whitewater Creek, and although I don't know what its acreage was, it was a good-sized farm with its tillable land located in the river bottoms with the remainder being timbered land in the foothills. There was no flood control associated with Whitewater Creek so, although it was normally only 25 or 30 feet across, the heavy rains that sometimes fell in the area during the spring season would cover the river bottom fields with a few feet of water. That occurred during our first spring at the farm, and Pete and I took advantage of the many opportunities that offered.

One of the opportunities we found most enticing was a chance to go boating. Since we had no boat, we improvised by using the sorghum pan, which was a wooden and metal rendering pan about 10 feet in length, 4 feet in width and 1 foot deep. By using poles to push us around in the water, which was only two to three feet deep, we had a great time. These good times came to a sudden end about a week later when one of our aunts with her children dropped by for a visit. When it became time for her to go home, she came to look for her children, who happened to be out with us in the boat. Upon hearing my father call for us, we pulled out of the woods and to the water's edge where they were standing. It was then I learned that sorghum pans were to be used only for the rendering of sorghum cane juices into sorghum. My father was a firm believer that if one spared the rod one spoiled the child.

It was on this farm that I was introduced to farming. When the floods receded and the land dried sufficiently, my father instructed me in the art of harnessing mules and attaching them to the front end of a plow. This plow, in order to be effective, required someone to walk behind it to hold it upright and control the mules pulling it by means of the reins attached to the bits in their mouths and to the individual behind the plow. It turned out I was to be that individual.

Much to my disappointment, it also turned out that workdays were from sunup until sundown. I had anticipated that a normal workday would have the same hours as a school day, but that turned out not to be true. It did turn out to be true that Sunday was still considered a day of rest, and until I had completed about three weeks of on-the-job training and physical conditioning behind the plow, I took full advantage of that opportunity to do so.

Spring is a great time of the year in southeast Missouri, as all nature seems to come to life. All of the hills on the farm and the surrounding area were still forested and were breaking out in greenery, which was complemented by the many hundreds of white-flowered dogwood trees scattered throughout. The farm was rather remote from civilization, so rabbits, squirrels, raccoons, possums, foxes, and other wildlife were in abundance. Equally plentiful were snakes in many varieties. Copperheads, cottonmouth, black snakes, kingsnakes, garter snakes and many other varieties could be found in the woods, the fields, and along the banks of Whitewater Creek, which bordered one side of the farm.

For reasons that make no sense to me today, I felt it was my responsibility to dispatch all snakes I came across to their happy hunting grounds. This I accomplished by means of any club that I could find in the vicinity. In the wooded areas there was no shortage of such weapons, but in the open fields they were scarce. Since the vast majority of the snakes in open fields were nonvenomous, such as black snakes and blue snakes, I often chased after them, stepping on their tails to slow them down until I could come across a weapon. When I stepped on their tails they would immediately stop and coil. When this happened, if I didn't get off their tail quickly enough, they would coil around my leg. Since many of these snakes were 5 or 6 feet long and as big around as my arm, I'm sure my kicking and jumping in my efforts to separate from the snake would have impressed any athletic coach.

With incidents as cited above to break the monotony, and because many of the snakes were discovered by plowing them from the ground, plowing the fields became much more interesting and I became much more proficient. Before long I was plowing around two acres per day, which was considered a good day's work for a fully grown man. I don't recall exactly how long we stayed on this particular farm, but I'm sure it was only 10 or 11 months before we moved to another nearby. My experiences on this farm were very similar to those at the first except that the farmhouse had more wooded area nearby.

This area proved to be a treasure trove. It must have been inhabited by very large numbers of Indian tribes in earlier years, as there were literally thousands of arrowheads to be found in the area, many of them absolutely perfect flint arrowheads that must have been fired by Indians in their hunting and combat activities over a period of hundreds of years. Although I spent most of my time either in school or farming activities, I spent much of what free time I did have roaming the woods searching for arrowheads. I found hundreds, most of which I stored in containers which I then buried as treasure. Although I always located a marker to help me retrieve these treasures, all of this occurred some 85 years ago and I'm sure many, if not all, of my markers have been removed or are grown into larger trees. I would truly love to be able to rediscover some of them.

An amazing thing happened to me about this time. I was in the sixth grade and 11 years of age and all girls had seemed to be about the same to me. While some of the more athletic ones would sometimes join the boys in active games during school recess periods, basically I preferred to play with boys because we were the better players of basketball and baseball than the girls that I went to school with.

I had never really paid any attention to what girls looked like and had yet to discover that one could suddenly be so much more attractive than any other girl I had known. It happened to me while our family was returning from a trip to Cape Girardeau and was traveling by a different route on our return home than we normally did. Six or seven miles before we arrived home, we had car trouble, which, as I recall, was a flat tire. While we had the car up on jacks and the tire removed for repair, I happened to notice someone approaching on a bicycle. As the cyclist drew near, I could see that it was a young girl around my age and she was attractively dressed in very becoming shorts and she was very pretty. That's the first time I had ever thought of a girl in terms of looks. This was a first for me. Although she waved as she passed us, she was soon out of sight but not out of my mind. Little did I know our paths would cross again in the not-too-distant future. A couple of other events occurred before this was to happen.

Evidently my father had gotten into a very serious disagreement with another farmer who lived near the farm where we had previously lived. I have absolutely no idea what the argument was about, but the road from where he lived to the town of Whitewater passed directly in front of our home, and one day, when he was on his way home from Whitewater by horse and wagon, he saw my father in our front yard and halted his team when he drew near the place where my father was standing. He motioned my father over, and they immediately lit into each other verbally, with both threatening violent physical retribution if and when the man got down from his wagon. Inasmuch as this man was about one and a half times the size of my father and a very rough-looking man, I was convinced that he would probably kill my father. I probably weighed 70 or 80 pounds at this time, and I didn't feel that I could physically compete with the 250-pounder who was on the other side of the argument. I therefore quietly slipped away, went into my father's room and retrieved his 12-gauge shotgun, which I loaded with double-aught buckshot. I had used this gun for squirrel hunting and was quite well qualified in its use.

I slipped out the door of the house and concealed myself behind some large bushes in our front yard and assumed a prone shooting position on the ground about 30 or 40 yards from the site of the confrontation. I did this without being observed by anyone, and throughout the remainder of the argument had the gun zeroed in on the ex-neighbor with the full intent to shoot him if he got down off of the wagon.

Fortunately, after a short period of time he drove on without getting off the wagon and unknowingly saved his life and me from making a horrible mistake when I was only about 10 years of age. My mother had observed my leaving the site of the argument and asked me later if I was afraid to fight. I never confessed to her or my father how close I came to committing murder.

The other event that I remember quite well was the harvesting of a field of sorghum cane and conversion of it to sorghum molasses. First we had to cut the cane down, strip it of all its leaves, and squeeze all of the juice out of the cane before placing it in the sorghum pan (the boat that I have mentioned earlier), and boiling the sweet juices down until they became molasses. The interesting part was getting the juice out of the cane, which was accomplished by harnessing a team of mules and attaching them to the end of a 25- or 30-foot pole attached on the other end to a press that squeezed the cane into dry fiber, with the juices being collected beneath the press. Halters of the mules were attached to another slender pole of the same length, which kept them constantly pulling in a circle.

When the molasses was considered to be of the desired

density, it was poured into 50-gallon oak barrels which were sealed and placed in the smokehouse for storage pending their use in the months to come. I don't know how anyone decided when the juices had been distilled enough, but I do remember when the winter months came it was difficult to retrieve the molasses through the spigot installed for that purpose. You could literally cut the molasses with a knife. I do recall, however, it really tasted good on pancakes and was quite popular with the younger people during the winter months at taffy pull parties.

I believe it was in the spring of 1928 that we made another move to a wonderful farm just a few miles from where we had been the last year or so. As I recall, it was a farm of about 165 acres, most of which was under cultivation or pasture. Although we only had 15 or 20 acres of wooded land, our neighbors collectively had hundreds of acres of forested land which was available to all for hunting. The house was one of the largest in the area with very large rooms, many of which suited a family of our size just fine. There was a veranda that stretched across the entire front of the house, which was approximately 75 feet long. There was a small orchard with apples, peaches, and plums and a terrific pear tree in the side yard next to the orchard. A very short distance behind the house was a large vegetable garden, and to the right of that on the other side of the fence was a large chicken house.

The barn and workshops were constructed of hand-hewn logs and predated the Civil War by many years. The workshops were of the same construction. The property was owned by two elderly sisters who lived in Whitewater, and I believe our father must have leased it from them, as we never shared any produce from the farm.

During the 10 years or so that we lived there, our father was employed as a railroad engineer by the Marquette Cement Company, which was the largest business located in the Cape

Girardeau area. Of course, this necessitated that practically all of the farming had to be accomplished by my brother Pete and me.

Pete was two years younger than me, and this was his initiation into the labor force. Our primary crops were corn and wheat, but we also raised enough potatoes and yams to meet our family needs during the winter months. Our mother always canned enough vegetables and fruit to last the winter, so with the exception of sugar, salt, and coffee, we were pretty well self-sufficient, as we traded wheat for flour with the local miller in Whitewater.

ONE-ROOM SCHOOLHOUSE

The little one-room schoolhouse, which accommodated all students from the first through the eighth grade, was located approximately 500 yards from my home, which greatly simplified getting to school in wintry weather when everything was snowed in. Living closer to the school than any other family also afforded me my first opportunity for paid employment. Miss Nora Deneke, who lived a mile or so from the school, was the teacher, and she offered me the job of providing janitorial services to the school. My duties required me to remain after school every day, dust the erasers and clean the blackboards, spread oiled sawdust over the floor and then sweep it up after having cleared the room of all debris left by the students.

The entire room was heated during the winter months by a small potbellied stove located in the center of the room. It was fueled by wood provided by the local farmers, and in the winter months my janitorial job included splitting kindling and starting a fire an hour or so before school convened so that the room would be warm for all. Sometimes the temperature outdoors was

20° below zero. For the services provided as outlined, I was paid one dollar per week, which I considered a princely sum at that time. I also considered it a pretty soft job as compared with the 16 hours or so that I worked each day during summer months, for which I received no salary. Grown men putting in the same hours as I did during summer months received one dollar a day.

As best I recall, there were 30 to 40 students in this little school, spread more or less evenly across the eight grades therein. This was my seventh year in elementary school and Miss Deneke was a very nice lady (rather elderly it seemed to us students), although, in actuality, I'm sure she was no more than 25 to 30 years of age.

There were six or seven boys approximately my age scattered among the sixth, seventh and eighth graders, but the student I found to be most interesting was the little girl I had seen on the bicycle the summer before. She seemed to be as interested in me as I was in her, and within the first week of school I had ensured that she and my sister Neit, who was two years older than me, were fast becoming best friends. As brothers and sisters should, Neit and I often accommodated each other in helping to meet other young people we found of interest.

The young lady I found of interest was named Ella May Green, and she was in the sixth grade. For the next two years any event that included a mix of boys and girls found Ella May and me paired together. Since I was one grade ahead of her in school, I left for high school the year before she did and since we went to separate high schools, we both went our separate ways.

The only girl I have met since then—including many Miss Americas, Miss Worlds, and movie stars—I thought to be more beautiful than Ella May is my wife Sally, who was Miss Florida Citrus of 1940 and whom I married in June 1941. However, during my seventh and eighth grade years, Ella May was the young lady of my choice.

Other than the parties hosted by students in their homes, the most popular for both parents and students seemed to be what was labeled as a "Box Supper." There were two or three of these each school year, and they consisted of entertainment provided by the student body and the eating of a boxed meal prepared by the female students (obviously with the assistance of their mothers), which were auctioned off after the entertainment ended and sold to the highest bidder, who then had the privilege of dining with the young lady who had presented the box for auction.

These boxes were magnificent things to behold. All of them were covered by decorative paper and had ornaments of various types attached for beautification. There were no names attached to the boxes indicating who had prepared them, and theoretically, no one knew in advance who their partner would be until he opened the box.

In actuality, the identity of the young girls presenting the dinners for bid had been determined in one way or another before bidding began. In my case, I always knew which dinner Ella May had prepared because she always told me in advance. Once I placed a bid, everyone in the audience also knew, and the older boys who finished school a year or two earlier and had jobs paying them up to a dollar a day could make it difficult for those with less financial resources. However, Ella May had let it be known that she would refuse to eat with anyone but me, so other than forcing the price up a little, no harm was done, and the boxes could normally be bought for around a dollar. The exception was when the older boys were bidding against each other, the price sometimes reached 3 or 4 dollars, which seemed a tremendous amount at that time. All monies received went into a fund to support school activities. The entertainment provided by the students prior to the auction consisted of short skits, songs, dancing, or playing musical instruments.

In those days, there was complete segregation in all

schools, and a black student never attended a school I was in from the first grade through college. As a result, we were not sensitive to race relations. To this date, I still feel bad that, as small children, we were raised in a society that was still denying equal rights to some of our citizens. That situation continued to exist throughout my elementary, high school and collegiate schooling.

Athletic facilities provided for the one-room school-houses in most cases consisted of a basketball court outlined by chalk lines on the ground with a goalpost at each end. We all made great use of these and periodically played other similar guest schools from the relatively small geographical area. While the dirt floors probably prevented many skinned knees, it did not protect us from all injury. To this day, I still have a fingernail on the middle finger of my left hand that bears the evidence of having been stepped on by hobnailed shoes during a scuffle for the ball.

Miss Deneke only served as our teacher for one year before she was transferred. Our new teacher was a young man who lived not very far from where we did and was known as "Red Bloomberg." Mr. Bloomberg was somewhere in his early twenties at the time and was probably the best teacher I had during 16 years of formal schooling. To meet him was to like and admire him. He was a great teacher who ensured that his students received the maximum education possible under the circumstances. He supervised and improved athletic capabilities during recess and after school, and he inspired us to continually strive for goals that were often considered beyond the possibilities of the times. He always presented a happy disposition, and when a student was not feeling completely up to par you could recognize that he took it into consideration in his demands on us.

I recall very well that during the final examinations for graduation, I was suffering from a very painful boil in my ear.

Mr. Bloomberg was aware of this and during the course of the various exams he approached my desk and whispered in my ear, "Seth, I know your ear is very painful, so maybe this will make you feel a little better, you made 100% on your final math exam." Needless to say, it did. Some 40 years later when he was in a visitors group at NORAD headquarters, we had a chance to reminisce during a dinner at my home. While I entertained many visitor groups while serving as commander of NORAD, I can't recall one that I enjoyed more.

Once school let out in early springtime, all boys my age and above immediately became full-time, 6-day-a-week farmers. The main crops grown in southeast Missouri in those days were wheat and corn in our area and cotton about 30 miles south of us. We usually planted approximately 30 to 40 acres in corn and a somewhat smaller acreage in wheat. The corn was planted in the springtime as early as possible after temperatures remained above freezing level with the hope it could be laid by (final cultivation) the Fourth of July. Once laid by, the corn needed no further attention until the fall after it had fully matured.

Since we raised what was known as winter wheat, we had a break of a couple of months or so before it was necessary to prepare the fields for the seeding of wheat. We put approximately the same acreage in wheat as we did in corn. Once the winter wheat was sown, it required no further attention until around July of the following year, when it would be harvested and threshed. In preparation and planting of these two crops, the fields had to be plowed, and that's where I spent much of my time in the early spring and summer. This was accomplished by attaching a team of horses or mules to the front end of the plow with use of single-trees and double-trees and putting someone (in this case me) behind the plow. At this point in time there were no tractors on the farms anywhere near us. Since two acres were about the maximum an adult could plow in one day between daylight and dark, this required me to spend 30 to 35 days behind the plow and required walking 25 to 30 miles per day.

After the fields were plowed, it was necessary to pulverize the topsoil by harrowing. This was much easier, as it permitted me to stand on the harrow to provide additional weight to push the harrow teeth deeper into the soil. Although all the walking while plowing would have me in great physical shape, I was always happy to ride. Fortunately, the planters for both corn and wheat did have a seat for the operator, as did the corn cultivator and the wheat binder.

The harvesting of the wheat was one of my favorite activities in mid-to-late summer. This was accomplished with the use of a binder, which cut the wheat and tied it into bundles approximately a foot in diameter. These bundles were dropped off the binder as the wheat was cut, which necessitated that they be manually collected and collectively shocked for further curing prior to being threshed to recover the grains of wheat. These shocks consisted of 15 or 20 bundles each and would remain for a few weeks before the threshing season started. This gave plenty of time for rabbits and snakes to establish a home in the stacks and provided fun and excitement when it was time to load the bundles on wagons for transport to the threshing machine.

Since I always drove a wagon collecting the bundles, I had many snakes, practically all nonvenomous, tossed up to me by pitchfork from the people on the ground. My job was to arrange the bundles on the wagon in order to haul a maximum load, which required handling the bundles manually. Even though I knew the snakes were nonvenomous, my antics disengaging myself from a five foot or six foot black snake provided great entertainment for those on the ground. The rabbits all had no difficulty escaping.

All the local farmers raising wheat banded together in

cooperative fashion during threshing time, and there were probably a dozen or so in our cooperative. The threshing was done by independent operators who spent the entire summer threshing wheat from the central United States to the Canadian border. Their equipment normally consisted of a large tractor and a big threshing machine.

The tractor was used to tow the machine from farm to farm, and the flywheel on the tractor was used to drive a long leather belt that connected it to the threshing machine once they had been positioned. The farmers paid the threshing company according to the number of bushels produced. Sometimes steam engines were used instead of tractors, but they were relatively rare in our community until my father and a neighbor jointly purchased a steam engine and threshing machine to provide threshing service to many farms in our area. My father, being a railroad engineer, enjoyed operating the steam engine, and I enjoyed driving the water wagon that continually replenished it, and hauling the wood to fuel its fire.

There were two things I particularly enjoyed at threshing time, one being the food that was provided to those of us doing the work. Most of the farmers in our area were of German ancestry, and their wives were all excellent cooks. These wives would all assemble at the farm where threshing was being accomplished and jointly prepare food that we would eat. Since we were all working constantly for 12 hours or so each day, we were burning thousands of calories and were always hungry.

In addition to the noontime meal that they would prepare, there would be a morning brunch around 9:30 or 10:00 each morning, dinner (lunch) around 12:30, and an afternoon brunch around 3:30 or so. These ladies would try to outdo each other in the amounts and varieties of food they could provide. The food was served family style, and they never ran out of seconds, thirds and fourths. For dessert, there would always be three or four kinds of cake and three or four kinds of pie, particularly at the morning and afternoon brunches.

I was a twelve to eighteen year old boy during the summers who only weighed around 128 pounds as a senior in high school, and I suspect that I was eating seven or eight thousand calories per day without gaining an ounce. Another thing I liked about threshing was getting paid; although I never received pay for working at home, it was customary that all assisting neighbors during threshing be paid the princely sum of one dollar per day. Since I was doing as much or more than any grown man involved in threshing activity in our neighborhood, I was included among those receiving pay.

Younger boys could serve as water boys and receive 25 to 50 cents per day for carrying water to those working in the fields. When the threshing was occurring at our home, I was sometimes assigned the duty of bagging the grain at the rear of the threshing machine as it was threshed. The wheat was bagged in burlap bags that held about 100 pounds of wheat. As I recall, there were always two men involved in this, and our duties also required that we carry the bags to the granary where it would be stored. This was tremendous muscular training for a growing boy, and I became very strong, which later on led me to take up wrestling.

As I said earlier, threshing was one of my favorite farming activities, and I still remember the names and faces of many of the neighbors involved. Since this took place some 80 plus years ago, I don't believe any of them are still living. I remember one that I visited each year when I went back to Missouri to visit family until he passed away some three or four years ago. His name was Clem Gartung.

Clem had bought the farm we lived on when I was a boy, and it adjoined the one he had inherited from his father. I had thought we were in the same grade while in school, but he tells me he was one year behind me. My visits with Clem were highlights of my visits to Missouri, and I sorely miss seeing him now. Clem died in his early 90s.

HIGH SCHOOL

In the spring of 1930, I completed my grammar school education, and although my summer farming activities would not change in the near future, my days in the one-room schoolhouse were over. Most farm children upon completion of the eighth grade were finished with their formal schooling. Very few went on to high school, and I do believe my sister Neit and I were the only members of our class that planned to continue on with our schooling. My little girlfriend (Ella May), who completed elementary school training one year after I did, was the only other student who continued on to high school. Most farmers and their wives of our prior generation had received an eighth-grade education or less, and they seemed to think that level of education was all the children needed in order to pursue a successful and happy life. Fortunately, my mother and father believed that further education would benefit me and my siblings. So we all continued on to high school, with a few of us also achieving a college degree.

As there were no school buses in those days, at least in

Missouri, the choices for my sister and me were rather limited and thus had to be located within walking distance of our home. The only high school that met that criteria was Whitewater High School, located in the small country town of Whitewater approximately 4 or 5 miles away.

Fortunately for us, Miss Deneke, who had been my seventh-grade teacher, was now teaching at grammar school in Whitewater, and my father made arrangements for us to ride in her car to and from school. That worked very well for my sister and well enough for me, as I had no problem walking home when I wanted to participate in after-school activities. The schoolhouse was a two-story brick building with seven or eight classrooms and a very small cadre of teachers.

Either the teachers were very unimpressive or I must not have applied myself very well, as I have absolutely no memory of any teacher when I was in the ninth grade. I do remember the principal (not his name) because one day during the noon hour he got into a fistfight with an 11th or 12th grader who was the son of the owner of the major country store in the very small town of Whitewater. The student who knocked the principal down was known to be very rowdy, and I had seen him at several country parties drinking bootleg whiskey and involving himself in disruptive activities. However, although the student named Lawrence was missing from school for a day or two, he soon returned, and nothing more was made of the incident. Perhaps the fact that his father was chairman of the school board might have had something to do with it.

The main thing I learned during my freshman year was that if I intended to get a good education, I would have to attend a different high school. Fortunately, I was able to convince my parents that such was the case, and they agreed that both my sister and I would enroll in Central High School located in Cape Girardeau, Missouri, a town of some twenty-five or thirty thousand, approximately 15 miles from my home. Since all the roads connecting our home to Cape Girardeau were of dirt only or gravel, they sometimes became difficult or even impossible to use in rainy or heavy snow conditions.

Although I was only 14 years of age, I had been driving for a couple of years or so (I don't believe a driver's license was required; at least, I didn't have one). The decision was made that we would live in Cape Girardeau during the week and go home on weekends. As my father had two married sisters living with their families in Cape Girardeau, he made arrangements with one of them for us to have rooms in the basement of their home. We were provided with minimal cooking facilities, and it was up to my sister and I to provide our own food, which we accomplished by bringing maximum loads of produce back with us from our weekend visits to the farm.

My aunt Nellie, with whom we were living, had recently divorced her second husband and was living with her daughter named Delphine and her son Lloyd. Delphine was a couple of years older than me, and Lloyd was a year or so younger. Delphine was a senior at Central High and going steady with a star on the football team named Elliott Seabaugh, so we didn't see too much of her. Either Elliott or his best friend, with whom they always double dated, owned a car with a rumble seat, and most evenings that car was in evidence around my aunt's home. Such cars were very popular with young people in the early 1930s and were the envy of many of their fellow students. Lloyd was still in grammar school, although we saw him in the evenings. All of his friends were still in grammar school. Aunt Nellie's home was located on South Ellis in Cape Girardeau and was only a dozen blocks or so from Central High School. This, of course, was a short walk for Neit and me. Many students had to walk much further, for as I mentioned earlier, there were no school buses. The streetcars did pass directly in front of her home and were of great interest to me until I became accustomed to them.

Central High School was quite an improvement over what I had experienced at Whitewater. It consisted of a four-story building with a two-story annex where all choir, band, and orchestra activities took place. Although the main building appeared to be only three stories high, there was a fourth floor underground at the front of the building that became ground-level with a walkout at the same level as the athletic fields due to the slope the building was constructed on. This floor contained the basketball court and its bleachers, the locker rooms and showers for both boys and girls, and other rooms for such activities as wrestling. Although all interschool football matches took place in the college stadium, there was a full-scale football field laid out for practice purposes behind the building, with a cinder track around it.

Central High School had a great faculty of highly qualified teachers, and there were 30 of them to provide instruction to the approximately 600 plus students enrolled. Our principal, Mr. Louis J. Schultz, was very popular with all teachers and students, and in later years the school was named after him. Many of the teachers made a great impression on me and provided guidance that served me well in college and later life. One of the most memorable among these was my history teacher, Miss Naomi Potts.

Ms. Potts was, it seemed to me, a rather elderly lady who very early on motivated me to believe I could achieve any goal in life that I desired if I applied myself. I still recall the afternoon she asked me if I could stay after class and talk with her. Of course, I said yes. After all other students had left the room, she asked me to be seated and then came down from behind her desk and seated herself across the aisle from me. She asked me to tell her about my family, my upbringing to date, and my goals in life. We talked for about 30 minutes about my ancestors, my siblings, and my ambition to become a doctor, which was a goal that my father had picked for me many years earlier.

I still remember, when she asked me what kind of doctor, I couldn't remember the word *pediatrician*, so I replied, "baby doctor." After we had finished, she thanked me and said "Seth, with your heritage, abilities and accomplishments to date, there is nothing in this world you can't achieve if you work for it. You could have a great future ahead of you." Of course, I left the room walking on cloud nine, and she immediately became my favorite teacher, and I determined that I would do my very best to prove to her that I could apply myself. As years went by, it occurred to me that she probably held the same session with every student in her class and provided the same evaluation of their future as she did for me. Be that as it may, she still motivated me to believe in myself and trust my judgment, as I did many times in the following years when my decisions affected many people.

Another favorite teacher of mine was my Latin teacher Miss Krueger. She was one of two sisters who were both teachers, and to the best of my knowledge neither had ever been married, although they were now, as was Ms. Potts, at least in their fifties. While Ms. Krueger never made an overt attempt to motivate me in all matters as did Ms. Potts, I studied Latin under her tutelage for three years, and although I'm sure my application to my studies under her probably left something to be desired, she managed to stuff enough Latin in my head that I found it rather easy in the future to understand the meaning of most English words. It also assisted me with other languages.

I also liked Coach Robinson, who was in charge of all athletic teams, individual athletes, and PE for all male students. I got to know him rather well when he organized a wrestling team and I became one of its members. My parents considered me to be too small to participate in football and other contact sports, as I only weighed 128 pounds, and refused to let me compete to become a member of the football or basketball squad. It was in the fall of my senior year that the wrestling team was activated, and without notifying my parents, I decided I would try for out the team.

Because of my years of working on the farm, I was very strong for my size. Also, my grandfather McKee, who had always liked boxing and wrestling (my father had told me many stories concerning my grandfather's readiness to demonstrate his boxing skills anytime he felt it was necessary), was always matching me against my brother Pete and cousin Lloyd, who were two years and one year younger than me, respectively, in a wrestling match. They each weighed approximately the same as I did, and of course, he always made me take them both on at the same time. Contrary to my brother and cousin, I was always eager to participate, as I could beat the two of them without too much difficulty. Coupled with other encounters with school-mates, this gave me confidence that I could be competitive.

This turned out to be true in school as well, as I was able to defeat all opponents through the 148-pound class (welterweight). I wrestled with this weight class in high school and in my military competitions in the National Guard. Although I gave away 20 pounds to my opponents in every match, I never lost one. Somewhere I still have a blue ribbon medal that was presented to me when I won the division championship during summer National Guard maneuvers.

Also in high school, I soon noticed there were a great many pretty girls, and a lot of them wanted to be friendly. However, not having any spending money to speak of, or a car, my social activities were largely limited to parties hosted in private homes or by school activities. I did find one young lady who was very attractive and very popular in school, who seemingly accepted me as I was, and we had a lot of fun dancing together at the various parties. Also, when the weather was nice, I tried to make myself available once school let out to carry her books home for her. That happened with regularity. Her name was Eva Vogel. The last time I can recall a date with Eva was 4 July 1934, and that date was more or less happenstance, although it's very difficult for me to remember any date in high school and college years that I enjoyed more.

Cape Girardeau always had a big celebration at the fairgrounds on the Fourth of July, which started with the noon picnic followed by baseball games and great fireworks displays at dusk. Throughout all the time these events were going on, there was a big band playing dance music at the fairgrounds clubhouse, which had a dance floor about twice the size of a basketball court.

My parents and all my brothers and sisters and I were picnicking, and I happened to see that Eva and her family were doing the same nearby. As soon as all had completed their luncheon picnic, I went over to Eva's location and asked her to dance. From that point on, I think we danced every number that was played until the band ceased that evening. That was long before the days of air conditioning, and in accordance with customs of the time, I was wearing a jacket. Needless to say, I nearly melted away, as we liked to jitterbug, do the shag, and many other fast dance steps. I can't remember having more fun any other time during my high school and college years.

As I was one year ahead of Eva in school, we drifted apart when I entered college the following year. I recall, however, being seated across the table from Eva at a social function some 75 years later, and I asked her if she remembered our Fourth of July dance marathon, and she said she did. I hope her memories were as pleasant as mine.

☆☆☆☆

Another activity I enjoyed in high school was participation in the theatrical club activities. I had roles in several plays whose names I cannot recall. However, I do remember having the lead role in *Andy Hardy* as Andy several years prior to the time it was made into a movie in Hollywood. This was a three-act play, and it was presented to public audiences in the school auditorium. All in all, I think we were pretty well-received, as many favorable comments were received both orally and through the media.

Another club I joined was the boys cooking club. It was quite a group of us, and we met quite often. I suspect the motivation for many of the members was the same as mine. We were provided with the raw materials for whatever our sponsor decided we would cook and then shown how to fix it. The best part, and the reason I joined it, was that we got to eat the results of our cooking efforts. Since my dinner normally consisted of what either my sister Neit or I prepared, these meals provided a welcome variety.

Finally, in the spring of 1934, graduation day arrived, and before a large audience including our parents, both Neit and I walked across the stage and received our certificates of graduation. This was considered quite an accomplishment in those days because students proceeding beyond the eighth grade were practically nonexistent in farm families.

COLLEGE

The summer of 1934 once again found me performing the same farming activities as I had the preceding summers, and it became time for my parents and me to decide where and how my further education was to be pursued.

No one in our extended family had ever attended college, with the exception of my grandfather, who, among several other occupations, was a schoolteacher back in the 1800s and attended Cape Normal. This institution was later renamed Southeast Missouri State Teachers College and many years later once again renamed Southeast Missouri State University.

At the time I graduated from high school, this was the only institution of higher learning close enough and within the financial resources available for me to consider. Of course, I was only 17 years of age at this time, and in retrospect I'm sure this decision was made in large part by my parents.

In 1934, there were no government assistance funds of any kind to provide for higher education for those desiring it, so either the parents had to fund all expenses involved or students had to find employment, which, with support from parents, made enrollment possible. Fortunately, tuition costs at the teachers college were very low, and my father, who delegated much of the farming activities to my three younger brothers while he held down a job as a railway engineer, was able to pay all tuition and books costs involved as well as rental of a room for me, as he had in high school. Once again, foods were available for me to bring from home, and during the first year in school, I managed to survive on that.

Early in my sophomore year, I joined the Missouri National Guard and also got a job in a service station that provided sufficient funds for me to eat well and participate in many social activities. I was employed by a Mr. Hinds, who owned a number of service stations in the southeast Missouri area. He and his wife were very kind to me, and in addition to always giving me a little extra money each week, he and his wife treated me to dinner in their home on several occasions.

The service station I worked in was located on North Main Street next to the Mississippi River on a site that I believe is now occupied by a gambling casino. Since I was going to school in order to pursue a medical career, one of my first tasks was to ensure that the courses I enrolled in would provide a bachelor's degree that would make me eligible to apply for medical training. This dictated that in addition to prerequisites for all degrees, optional courses should be in the fields of science, math and languages. Fortunately, the heads of these three departments were outstanding in their field and had been instructing for many years.

The head of the math department was Professor Johnson, behind his back fondly known as "Peggy Johnson" due to a crippled limb. Professor Johnson had been teaching since the 1890s, and I had a class under him in every semester the three years I attended school there. I still remember that he called the student roll every day and never looked up from the roster he was calling from. He would call out the name and the student would answer "present." As he never looked up from his roster while calling the roll, there were very seldom absentees, although occasionally there was a slight delay in response from the student.

There was also rumor that he awarded grades on a curve that he established by throwing final examination papers down the stairwell from the second floor where his classroom was located. The story was that those near the top received As and others further down received grades commensurate with their position in the stairwell. I'm not sure this is true, as I don't believe all mine could have ended up so far down the steps every time.

The head of the science department was Professor Magill, who was a highly talented and effective teacher ahead of his time in many of the sciences. I remember in 1934 and 1935 he was telling us about the breaking down of the atom by centrifugal force and the impact such an achievement would have on the world. There was a centrifuge running in Chicago at that time, and he was closely monitoring its results. That was approximately 10 years before scientists were able to package it as a weapon system in 1944/1945. Of course, the applications that he discussed with us were not weapon systems but generating power for peaceful applications. For my three years in attendance under his tutelage, I studied chemistry, biology, and put in several semesters of laboratory work. I enjoyed all of his courses, and he was later honored, as one of the major university buildings was named Magill Hall.

My language teacher was Miss Helen Cleaver. I took one semester of French and one of German under Ms. Cleaver, and although I'm sure I didn't apply myself as well as I should have, I did retain enough for it to be quite useful in Europe during and after World War II. My English teacher was Professor Martha Shea, who had been teaching since 1906 and was very effective.

She was very quiet, and all students were quite fond of her.

I had another English teacher named Professor Grauel, under whom I had a course in public speaking. He had only been teaching since 1928 and was a relatively young man who mixed well with all the students. At one point in the semester of his class, each student had to prepare a speech which he or she would then make to the class, and each presentation was to take up the entire class period. The presentation could include a demonstration of something of interest, and I decided that I would wow them with my expertise in chemistry. It was not too long before my presentation that I had learned the formula for gunpowder in my lab studies and had been having a lot of fun with it in the laboratory. I decided that I would demonstrate to those in the classroom the procedure of making gunpowder and then prove that gunpowder was not a dangerous explosive unless it was packaged to be one. In other words, loose gunpowder in a dish would simply burn instead of exploding if it were to be set on fire.

All would have gone well had I remembered that, in the wintertime, all classroom windows were tightly closed and, unlike the laboratories, had no high-capacity exhaust fans. No one, including the professor, had been told the subject of my speech until I stood before the class. In my introductory remarks I advised them that I would demonstrate the making of gunpowder. I made no mention of what I planned to do with it. With explanation of the ingredients required and the methodology of combining said ingredients, I kept up a running commentary while shuffling beakers and dishes on the professor's desk I would be using for my demonstration. Due to the length required of our presentations I tried to make this last as long as possible, as I wasn't sure how much time would be taken up by my grand finale. Finally, I arrived at a point where I could procrastinate no longer, so I very carefully placed all of the gunpowder on a large open dish. The total volume was approximately a cup.

Without telling anyone what I was about to do, I quickly removed a package of matches from my pocket and after striking one tossed it into the dish of powder. Along with a few "yipes" from some of the girls in the class, the powder immediately flamed up and burned fiercely, creating a dense black cloud of smoke that seemed to fill the entire classroom immediately. Everyone was coughing and out of their seats trying to get the door to the hallway open. I immediately headed for the windows on one side of the classroom and with the help of some other male students and the teacher we managed to get them all open. With the door open and air coming out of the hallway, the smoke cleared rapidly, and students returned to the seats. However, it was very cold outside and now was too cold in the classroom. That being the case, Mr. Grauel dismissed the class.

I don't remember what grade I received for this escapade, but Mr. Grauel remained a friend, and I was told that he spoke highly of me much later during World War II. Although I don't really know what the students thought of my presentation, several of them spoke admiringly to me about my ability to get everyone out of class early.

Another person, although not a teacher, was Ms. Sadie Kent, the school librarian who had occupied that position since 1905. Sadie was a wonderful woman and a fantastic librarian who was always eager to help students in their pursuit of knowledge. Although the college had a rather extensive library, I cannot recall her ever being unable to walk directly to where the book was located without reference to the files when I requested her assistance in locating something. The library was always a quiet and restful place for students to pursue their studies, as Sadie would not tolerate it any other way. I was pleased to learn in later years the college had constructed a separate library building and named it after Ms. Kent.

☆☆☆☆

Although this school did not have a wrestling team, there were several boys in school who were interested in wrestling, and we worked out rather regularly on the mats provided for that use in the gymnasium. It was while wrestling there with one of the football players, who was about 75 pounds heavier than me, that we took a fall and my left elbow went between the mats that covered the concrete floor, breaking my elbow in the process. This of course slowed down my wrestling activities for two or three months and left me with a left arm that couldn't completely straighten. Fortunately, the arm remained straight enough that it was never noted in the hundreds of physicals that I was subjected to throughout my later life.

The school also had an Olympic-sized swimming pool in the basement of Academic Hall which I utilized on a rather regular basis, as swimming was one of my favorite sports. These activities, coupled with the extensive walking I did that was necessitated due to my lack of a car, managed to keep me in pretty good physical condition.

Another favorite activity of mine that contributed to this end was dancing. The only dormitories the college boasted at the time I was there were Albert Hall and Leming Hall, and both of these dormitories were for female students only (male students had to fend for themselves in the city). The only college girls I dated during my three years of college at Cape lived in these dormitories, and every afternoon their downstairs parlors could be utilized by girls living there to entertain their male friends. This was usually accomplished by dancing with them to the music of the big bands of that era whose recordings were con-stantly playing on the radio.

The girl I dated on a more or less steady basis most of the time was named Leslie Mae Allen, and she was a fantastic dancer. She was also very popular with all the boys, and several of our leading athletes were continually trying to cut me out of the pattern. I was able to convince Leslie Mae that I was unwilling to share her company with others. She must have read a little more into this than I intended. She was a year behind me in school, and when I was in flying school, between her junior and senior years, she and my sister Neit came down to pay me a visit at Randolph Field. They spent about a week there, and since I had completed primary training by that time, I had a little more time free that I could spend with them. Other than bumping into her briefly a couple of years later, that was the end of our association. During my sophomore and junior years, we did have a lot of fun at all the dances and other school activities. I learned many years later during a homecoming at the university that she is now deceased.

I dated a few other girls during my stay in Cape, but the only one that I dated steadily for a period of time besides Leslie Mae was a senior in high school who was also a very good dancer. Her name was Lydia Ashley, and she was the sister of a college classmate that was a good friend of mine.

NATIONAL GUARD

It was during my sophomore year in 1935 that I first entered the military service. One of my closest running buddies in school was a fellow named John Watts, who was from Sikeston, Missouri, a cotton-growing center about 30 miles south of Cape Girardeau. John was one class ahead of me in school and had been a member of the National Guard for a year or so. John was quite enthusiastic about the Guard. He convinced me it would be a good idea to join the National Guard Company which was stationed in Cape Girardeau.

This company was the headquarters company for an infantry battalion and was composed primarily of World War I-era veterans, with only very few younger men. The company drilled monthly in an armory located above the Broadway Theatre in Cape Girardeau, which was used at other times as a public dance hall. In addition to the monthly training requirements, every summer the unit would be called to active duty for a two-week period and would join all the other units within the division or corps area to which it was assigned for maneuvers and training. This company (Headquarters Co., 140th Infantry) was commanded by Capt. Herb Wickham, whose peacetime job was chief of police of Cape Girardeau.

Since I didn't know the procedures for joining the guard, I decided to see if I could talk to Chief Wickham. When I arrived at the police headquarters, I didn't have to wait too long before the chief could see me, but things didn't look too good at first, as he stated he only had one vacancy. However, when he discovered that I was a college student he became much more interested. Although he was almost fully manned, he did have an opening for a message center chief that he had been unable to fill because no one had been able to use the encoding and decoding devices at a speed that was acceptable to him, as most of the assigned enlisted personnel had very little education. He concluded our meeting by inviting me to the next drill session so that he could determine what my capabilities were with the encoding/decoding devices.

It was with great anticipation that I reported to Captain Wickham at the next drill session, and he presented me with the encoding devices and a brief explanation of how they worked. He then gave me a couple of documents to encode and a couple more to decode. Fortunately, I found it to be a very simple task that I could accomplish at a very high rate of speed, and Captain Wickham was delighted. He swore me in as a member of the Missouri National Guard and assigned me as message center chief of the company. Fortunately for me, this assignment called for the rank of corporal and provided me slightly higher pay than the majority of the troops who were only privates. I don't remember what pay was for a corporal in 1935, but I do remember that the pay for a private was $21 per month. That was for full-time active-duty pay and was drawn by the guard only when called to active duty. As best I can recall, pay for a drill was one dollar. This same evening, I was issued my equipment, which consisted of a .45-caliber pistol and a World War I uniform. The uniform consisted of britches with wrap leggings, a belt, a matching khaki shirt, shoes, and a campaign Smokey Bear-type hat. I could hardly wait to wear them at the next drill period.

While a member of the Guard, I never missed a drill night and made two summer encampments. The first was in the summer of 1936 at Nevada, Missouri, at division strength, and the second was in the late summer of 1937 at Fort Leavenworth, Kansas, at corps area strength. I thoroughly enjoyed the military activities at both, and won the welterweight wrestling championship of the division in 1936 and of the corp area in 1937. As Captain Wickham was a great sports fan, this didn't detract from our relationship.

During summer maneuvers, there was a lot of cross-country marching involved, as we were infantry, and 20-mile hikes with packs were not an uncommon thing. I remember one such hike in 1937 when the red and blue armies were pitted against each other (I can't remember what color army I was in), and we had marched many miles avoiding enemy forces and taking cover when the sound of aircraft was heard. I still remember that on this particular hike there appeared to be an unusual number of high-ranking officers passing by on the road we were traveling, and we, of course, saluted the senior officers as they passed.

I had never seen a brigadier general until one passed me that day in open car. I was still in awe of the star displayed by the flag attached to the front bumper when another car came by displaying two stars. Shortly thereafter another car passed displaying three stars, which of course had to be the corps area commander. Realizing something big must be happening, I was still standing there when I heard a sudden roar, looked up and had my first close-up look at a military aircraft. Actually, there were about six or eight of them, and we were obligated to dive into the ditch to avoid detection and theoretically destruction. However, I still recall lying on my back in the ditch and looking up at those beautiful aircraft with the pilots in their open cockpits with white scarves streaming in the breeze.

Although these aircraft were open cockpit, fixed landing gear biplanes, as were most other aircraft of the era, and I had no plans for a military career at that time, I told myself that the next time I went on maneuvers I would be one of the guys sitting in the cockpit in the breeze instead of one of those on the ground walking 20 miles in the hot dust below.

Since the maneuvers in Kansas were my second time in the field, I found I had a good many friends I had met the year before who were also involved in the Kansas maneuvers. One of them was a young fellow named Bobby Dover from Sikeston, Missouri, and we teamed up a few times after duty hours to determine what female attractions there were in Leavenworth, Kansas.

To our delight, we found that there was a lot of activity, including dances where you could meet local girls. It didn't take Bob and me long to meet a couple of nice young ladies who liked to dance but told us their mothers did not permit them to date soldiers. Fort Leavenworth was a large army base of several thousand soldiers permanently assigned. After we convinced them that we were just part-time soldiers and were basically just college students, they decided going out with us would be okay.

I can't remember the names of the girls, but I do remember that Bobby was quite an artist, and shortly after I joined the Army Air Corps, he joined Walt Disney in Hollywood and helped create many of the movies that Disney produced. Bobby and I would not cross paths again for 32 years. However, Herb Wickham provided me with a very fine letter of recommendation when I applied for appointment as a flying cadet.

In the fall of 1936, after my summer farming activities and my National Guard active duty in Nevada, Missouri, I was happy to return to Southeast for my junior year as a student. I knew by then that if I were to become a doctor, this would have to be my final year there, as there were subjects required for entry into medical school that were not available in Cape. This year rocked along more or less as the two preceding years had, with the exception that Lydia Ashley was my steady girlfriend for the last few months of the school year. In early spring of 1937, the Mississippi River flooded to historic heights, and much of southeast Missouri was covered by water. There was very little flood control at that time, and the streets of Cape Girardeau down near the river were under several feet of water, as was most of the farmland throughout the area. The Red Cross set up many shelters throughout the area, which were filled by inhabitants chased from their homes by the flood.

The National Guard was called to active duty to provide traffic control and security for these refugee shelters. Upper Broadway in Cape Girardeau was well out of reach of floodwaters, and the large multistory building recently vacated by Montgomery Ward was utilized as one of the shelters. The National Guard Company that I was assigned to was placed in charge of security of the Cape Girardeau area, and I was assigned guard duty at the shelter on Broadway. I remember that only females and small children were bedded down in the upper floors, and males were all restricted to the first floor. The only problem I can remember having with this arrangement was keeping husbands from going to the second floor where their families were located. However, I was armed with a .45-caliber pistol, and when one of these husbands or some other male became aggressive and tried to bluff me, I simply placed my hand on my holstered gun and received no further arguments. Although the gun was loaded, I had no intention of drawing it from its holster, and sincerely

54

hoped that my being armed would provide the necessary deterrence. Later in life, I worked very hard to help ensure that the same principle would deter nuclear warfare.

WESTWARD HO

When school let out in the spring of 1937, I still had not made any decisions concerning my further education. However, in the company of three other classmates, I had made plans to see a little more of the world. None of us had traveled far from home before, so we decided we would all hitchhike to California for the summer. I can only remember the name of one of these fellow students, and he was Mike Rowe, from a suburb of St. Louis. One of the others was also from St. Louis, and the fourth was from New Madrid, which is some 60 miles or so south of Cape Girardeau. Since four is not a good number to hitchhike as a group, we decided to split into two pairs. Mike and the other St. Louis student would choose their route and rendezvous with us in Los Angeles. My friend from New Madrid and I decided we would take the southern route.

Lydia had informed me that she wanted to drive me to New Madrid to meet my traveling partner, which she did, where we had an emotional parting after confessing our eternal love for each other. My partner was right on time at the intersection that branched off to New Madrid from the through highway to Memphis, as we had agreed. We each were equipped with a medium-sized suitcase that contained everything we felt we would need on our trip, so as soon as Lydia had headed back for Cape Girardeau, we stepped to the side of the highway leading toward Memphis and stuck our thumbs into the air. We had decided to take the southern route which led from Memphis, Tennessee west across Arkansas, Texas, New Mexico, and Arizona into California.

The first few vehicles passed us by, but we didn't have to wait too long until a truck came by and offered us a lift. This truck was going to Blytheville, Arkansas, which was about halfway to the intersection of the highway just west of Memphis where we would head west. In those days, people were not as reluctant to pick up hitchhikers as they later justifiably learned to be, so we didn't have to wait too long for our next ride. There was a major intersection west of Memphis Highway 61, which we were on, and the east-west highway which would take us to California.

All highways in those days outside major city limits consisted of two lanes, and only a very few were paved. Most of them consisted of gravel, and if you got off the main roads many were of dirt surface only. I don't recall what means of transportation got us from Blytheville to this major intersection.

This major intersection had service stations, restaurants, and overnight accommodations, so there were many vehicles passing through. One of them was either a Ford or Chevrolet four-door sedan of early 30s vintage that was occupied by a threesome consisting of a young man, a young lady, and a considerably older man. This of course left them with two empty back seats. After starting a conversation with them, I found that they were going all the way to California, and of course it looked like a golden opportunity to my partner and me. We informed

57

them we were also headed for California and were looking for a ride and wondered if it were possible for them to provide us a lift. After a quiet conference between the three of them, which we could not overhear, the young man of the trio asked if we could provide money to help buy gas, as they were very low on funds.

Although I'm confident my partner and I were even lower on funds than they were, after a brief consultation with each other we agreed we could come up with $5 each for a total of $10. Since the price of gasoline those days was somewhere between 10 and 15 cents per gallon that would probably buy 60 or 70 gallons of gasoline, and they agreed to the deal, so our transportation was all set with no need for further "thumbing."

I don't have any idea how many days it took us to make the trip, but I do know that we spent many nights on the road, and all of us slept in the car or on the ground outside the car. Usually the young couple slept in the car with the rest of us outside on the ground. The group we were with had enough blankets in the trunk of the car to make this possible. Once we passed Texarkana, Arkansas, it seemed to take forever to get across Texas, and we probably were driving over 40 or 50 miles an hour at the most, and the roads were not all that good. Eventually, though, we did arrive in El Paso, and while there, for the first time in my life I departed the United States and crossed the border into Juarez, Mexico.

The two things I remember most about this short visit were the innumerable young boys on the streets, and the food. As Juarez is a border city, most of the young people there and the public service people there speak some English, and we had little difficulty communicating with them. The young boys were all trying to sell something, with worthless trinkets, shoeshines, and their sisters being the primary offerings. Neither of us were interested in the trinkets or their sisters but we did let a couple of them who were working together talk us into having our shoes shined. Their price was 10 cents each, and although that seemed a little high in those Depression days, we both finally agreed. My friend was wearing black shoes, and I was wearing white shoes. The boys both did a good job, and our shoes finally looked respectable for the first time in many days.

When we offered our respective dimes in payment, they both said no, as the price was now 25 cents. This, of course, was 10 cents more than the price of a shine in the better shoeshine shops in the United States, and we considered this outrageous and insisted that they accept the 10 cents as bargained for. Again they said no and that if we didn't pay them the 25 cents that they would throw black shoe polish on my white shoes and white shoe polish on my friend's black shoes. We responded that if they did that, we would beat the daylights out of them and pour shoe polish over them. They must have believed us, as they accepted the agreed-on price with no further argument.

☆ ☆ ☆ ☆

In reference to the food, both my partner and I were very hungry and looking for something to eat. Neither of us had ever eaten Mexican food, and although the prices of everything as advertised appeared to be very reasonable, we didn't know what to order. Fortunately, a waiter in the restaurant we stopped in was very patient with us and explained the various foods listed on the menu. He informed us that most Mexican food was considered very spicy by most Americans, so he provided tastes of a few of them, all of which we found to be too spicy for us to eat. He then informed us that they had three kinds of soup, some of which were not quite as spicy as a food we had already tasted, so he provided us with tastes of soup. We found that, although it seemed very spicy to us, the mildest of the three was not too bad, so we had large bowls of that and rather enjoyed it. Today Mexican food is one of my favorites, and I like it spicy and eat it frequently.

From El Paso we headed west through New Mexico, and although we didn't see much else, we saw a lot of beautiful scenery. The same held true for southern Arizona until we reached Tucson. Tucson was a true western city, and the cowboys and Indians were there in great numbers and often in colorful dress. From Tucson we headed directly west toward Yuma, Arizona, and then San Diego, California. The desert between Tucson and Yuma was the first real desert I had ever seen up close. Somewhere about halfway between Tucson and Yuma we stopped and spent the night. The highway was a narrow two-lane highway paved with asphalt. We slept outdoors as usual and during the night were entertained by the coyotes, other night creatures, and the constant roar of trucks on the highway.

The next morning as we resumed travel, I noted that the highway appeared to be wearing a fur coat. In the 1930s the deserts of Arizona were teaming with millions of jackrabbits, and evidently when the nights chilled everything down these rabbits would hop up on the blacktop at night to sleep on the warm surface. Even in those days there was considerable trucking conducted between our larger cities, and this road was one of the main east-west roads at that point in time. What I was seeing was the tens of thousands of jackrabbits that had been squashed so flat by the trucks that they practically covered the highway for miles and miles. Although the flattened skins were all that we could see, I'm sure the coyotes appreciated the unlimited dinner that was provided for them without any effort on their part.

When we first crossed the California state line, things didn't look much different than they had in Arizona, but by the time we reached the outskirts of San Diego it looked as though we were in a completely different country. Never had I seen such a proliferation of beautiful flowers, palm trees, and other beautiful plant life. Furthermore, the closer to the coast we traveled, the prettier it became. I don't think we spent any time in San Diego, as we were eager to reach our final destination, which was Los Angeles. The main road at that time was along the beach, or near thereto, all the way from San Diego to Los Angeles, and the beautiful flowers and the swaying palm trees were in abundance throughout the entire trip.

When we reached downtown Los Angeles, our benefactors dropped us off, and we were on our own. My aunt Nellie, my father's sister, resided in Los Angeles and provided the contact point we had agreed upon for us to connect with our fellow classmates from St. Louis. I located a public phone and contacted my aunt, who informed me my St. Louis classmates had not contacted her as yet, and invited my traveling friend and me to proceed to her home, where she had room for us to stay until our friends made contact. Once they made contact, we planned to find accommodations for the four of us. We were very happy to accept this invitation, and with her instructions had no difficulty finding her home using the streetcar system which served most all areas of greater Los Angeles. As it turned out, we only had to stay with her for a couple of days before our friends called and stated that they had found a place for the four of us and were ready to move in if we were. In short order, we were united.

This was at the height of the Depression, and rooms were only 15 or 20 dollars a month in a good section of town. I don't recall exactly what we paid, but it couldn't have been much, as we didn't have much. One of our first tasks would be to find employment. They had reserved two rooms for us in Hollywood in a very nice neighborhood not far from the popular movie star watering hole called the Brown Derby. Also, our landlord said that Jean Harlow, one of the most prominent stars of the moment, lived only a block and a half or so down the street on the other side. To put frosting on the cake, Mike Rowe told me that he had spotted two very beautiful girls in our age bracket coming and going from a nice home on the other side of the street a couple of doors from us. So, we established our immediate priorities as being to get a job and then meet the girls, in that order.

We would be individually responsible for finding our own jobs, but we would draw straws to determine which one of us would be responsible for arranging for us to meet the girls who lived across the street. It was suggested we immediately determine who that individual would be. Mike volunteered to hold the four matches, one of which would be shorter than all others, for us to draw from. Although I have always suspected I was set up by the others, I was not too disappointed when I drew the short match. My two St. Louis friends had already arranged for employment for the summer through family connections (with Dun & Bradstreet) but my friend from New Madrid and I were strictly on our own. As all of us had planned to spend only two or three months in Los Angeles before returning to Missouri for the following school year, it was obvious to us that we stood little chance of getting jobs of any consequence.

We decided a research of want ads in the Los Angeles papers might be our best course of action. Accordingly, we immediately started researching want ads. It didn't take me long to discover an ad from a Broadway theater for three ushers. The pay offered and the hours involved appeared to be just about what I would need for room and sustenance with just enough left over for me to fully enjoy the many activities that I hoped to participate in. Since interviews for the jobs were to be conducted the next day, I planned to be there early.

The next day, I arrived at the theater about 15 minutes before interviews were to be conducted and discovered to my dismay approximately seven or eight hundred other young men were also there to apply for the same jobs. After a short period of time the doors opened and we were invited into a long, wide lobby and were instructed to fall into rows approximately three feet apart and remain standing. Then three or four executives of the theater started inspecting the applicants by marching down the rows and looking us over as military officers do when inspecting troops. As they went down the rows, they dismissed people until only about half of us were left. After a short break, those of us remaining were once again instructed to form rows. Again, the execs started looking us over again and dismissing about half. This process was repeated another two or three times until only about a dozen of us were left, and we were once again lined up. Then three of us were selected and the others were dismissed.

Throughout this exercise, I was practically holding my breath, as I wanted the job rather badly so that I could get on with my plans for summer fun, so I accepted the job offered. I don't remember what the salary was, but it was enough to meet my needs, and although I didn't pay too much attention to the movies shown (this later turned out to be a problem), I really did enjoy the stage shows, as many famous artists appeared and I would often be assigned duty as a stagehand, which made it possible for me to meet some of them. Many of them were leading actors and actresses of the 1920s and 1930s, both in the movies and on stage. Almost without exception, I found it to be very nice and easy to talk to them.

My friend from New Madrid did not find employment immediately, and within three or four days decided that he would no longer seek work, as he planned to return to Missouri at a little earlier date than the rest of us. He did want to get involved in our social adventures, however, so shortly after I found employment the four of us decided that it was time for me (because of the short straw I had drawn) to approach the young ladies living just a few doors down on the other side of the street to determine their interest in introducing us to the attractions of the greater Los Angeles area. Since our arrival, we had not seen any we considered more attractive than these, and certainly none that lived so conveniently nearby. Therefore, after having made myself as presentable as possible, I proceeded to cross the street and walk toward their house while my three friends anxiously observed my progress from our front porch.

All the homes on this street were rather large, with the house I was headed toward as one of the largest. All of them were equipped with front verandas. Climbing the steps, I crossed the veranda and rang the doorbell. To my delight, one of the young ladies we had admired from afar opened the door, and she was even prettier than I thought when I first saw her. Without wasting any time, I introduced myself and explained to her that, in company with three friends, I was in California for the summer between my junior and senior years in college, as were my friends. I informed her that we had noticed that she and another girl that we presumed to be her sister appeared to live here, and that I had been designated to make inquiries concerning their availability to introduce us to points of interests we as tourists might miss altogether, unless we had the aid of someone native to the area. This charming young lady responded by telling me her name and that she did indeed live in this house with her sister and her mother and father, and that she and her sister were students at UCLA. She then invited me in to meet her parents and her sister and explained the situation to them. After some questioning from her parents, they seemed to accept that I was just a rather brash young man and was indeed who I claimed to be. Since the girls were around my age, the parents didn't seem to be concerned and left the matter up to the girls. I suggested that the girls go with me to meet my friends who were waiting on our front veranda. After a short conference between the two of them, they agreed that would be a reasonable course of action. So, the three of us proceeded to return to the house where I lived with my friends.

Needless to say, my friends were all smiles when we arrived, and in short order we were all rather well acquainted.

The girls assured us they had many friends that we could recruit to join us if we so desired. We concluded our meeting by making dates to go to the beach the coming weekend, which could be reached by boarding streetcars within a city block of where we lived. It went all the way to the beach without having to change cars. I regret I cannot recall the names of these girls but that was the beginning of a delightful two months or so, where we made several trips to the beach and spent many evenings dining and dancing.

All too soon it was time to curtail these activities and make preparations to return to Missouri for summer National Guard encampment and preparation for my enrollment in college for my senior year. This schedule was moved up by a week or two as the result of my getting fired by one of the top managers of the theater, whom I had never met. As I may have mentioned earlier, all of us who served as part-time ushers were required to memorize the names and starting times of the movies we were showing. Since I spent much of my time in support of the live theater activities, I didn't check the theater movie schedules on a daily basis as I should have. We had just changed our movie schedules, and I hadn't taken the time to read them.

Therefore, when this executive asked me the starting time of a certain movie, I had to confess that I had no idea what time it would start. Although I had planned to quit the job within a week or two in order to return home, it was embarrassing to get fired. Although I never worked in movies again, I did learn a good lesson that applies to all our activities in life.

A week or so after leaving the theater business, I decided it was time to head back to Missouri. My friend from New Madrid had departed for home a few weeks earlier, as he never did obtain employment, and my St. Louis friends were remaining for a while longer. This, of course, meant that I would be by myself on the trip home. I didn't really mind, as I knew that a hitchhiker traveling alone stood a much better chance of hitching a ride than he did if he was traveling with a companion.

The first day I made it about halfway to San Francisco and spent the night at a small motel situated in the country. The next day I made it to Reno, Nevada, which was on the western edge of a very sparsely populated area with nothing between there and Salt Lake City but a lot of sand and isolation. There was very little auto traffic on the highway, and it was late in the afternoon. So about dusk I climbed the fence bordering the highway and slept on the ground with my head on my suitcase in the middle of the field. Fortunately, no rattlesnakes chose to join me that evening, and there appeared to be no large animals in the field posing a threat. Needless to say, I awakened rather early the next morning and after brushing myself off as best I could, I made it to a nearby service station where I could wash up a little.

I did manage to get enough rides the next day to get me to the western edge of the desert where I decided to spend the night. This was just a wide place in the road, and there was nothing there that I remember except a railway station and some switching yards. I noticed quite a few people around the rail yards and walked down that way. As I approached the yards it became obvious to me the people I had been looking at were hobos. There must've been at least 15 or 20 of them. They were all gathered near the train station, and as I got closer I noticed there was one younger fellow near them dressed differently (shirt and tie, as was I) and we immediately headed toward each other. This young man was about my age, and like me, had hitchhiked to the West Coast from somewhere back east for summer fun just as I had. He was on his way home and had been unable to catch a ride for a couple of days and decided to ride the rails from that point to Ogden, Utah, which was on the other side of the Great Salt Lake some 300 or 400 miles away.

Since the trains ran nonstop from where we were to Ogden, if you can get on the train without being detected by railway cops you were assured the through trip to Ogden. His greatest concern was the hobos, as he advised me that they were very dangerous people to be with on account of our age, and suggested that we team up for the forthcoming ride, which I was very happy to agree to. He suggested we forage for some weapons and we were lucky enough to find a couple heavy wooden clubs that appeared to be adequate to our needs.

My new friend and I were both traveling with suitcases, as compared with the hobos, who all had large bedrolls. Although my friend and I received several offers to share a bedroll we politely declined and spent the night sitting back-to-back on our suitcases with the clubs in our hands. We had learned a freight train would be passing through early in the morning and after switching in the yards to pick up some empty cars would proceed nonstop to Ogden, Utah.

Sure enough, around 5 or 6 o'clock the next morning a long freight train arrived and after switching around in the yards for 15 or 20 minutes proceeded east toward Ogden. With no interference from railway police or other authority no one had difficulty in getting aboard. My new friend and I jumped up into an open boxcar door and found ourselves with only two other passengers in the car, who caused us no problems on the trip to Ogden. Shortly after noon, we approached the western outskirts of a large city, which we determined to be Ogden.

As soon as we reached this point, the train slowed down to a very slow speed of some 5 or 10 miles an hour and just before we reached the heavily populated areas of the city we crossed over a beautiful river whose water looked refreshing and clean. Since we were covered with coal cinders and other filth, we agreed we should jump off as soon as our car passed over the east end of the bridge. We did this with no problem, and about five minutes later we were on the edge of the stream and stripping down for a much-needed bath. We saw no people or housing nearby, and in nothing flat we were in the river and I don't think I've ever enjoyed a bath more. In addition to the coal dust and other debris that was bothering us, we were in the heat of summer in the middle of a desert. After a refreshing 30-minute bath we climbed the shore, opened our suitcases and dried ourselves off with towels we both had, and dressed ourselves to proceed hitchhiking east.

We both put on suits with shirts and ties, knowing that would greatly enhance our chances of a ride. We also agreed we would make our way east individually, as that would also enhance the probability of a ride. As we were closing our suitcases in preparation for leaving, a police car drove up and two policemen approached us. They told us we had been reported for indecent exposure, and they would have to take us into the station. When we asked who had reported us, they pointed out a large house in a grove of trees about three quarters of a mile away on a hill. Whoever reported us would have had to be using binoculars.

We explained to the officers that we were so filthy after our train ride and thought the place where we bathed was so isolated that we would not be disturbing anyone. We explained who we were and that we were on our way home. They told us to get in the back seat of the car behind the screen, and although we couldn't hear what they said, we saw they were talking to each other in quiet voices as we left the river. They continued driving through Ogden and on east until we came to the easternmost side of Ogden. There they stopped the car near a string of filling stations on the edge of town and invited us to disembark. After we did get out of the car, they rolled down a window and said, "Make sure you head east, boys, and good luck." With that they turned to go back toward town.

☆☆☆☆

Gasoline service stations, at least in those days, were the best places for a hitchhiker to catch a ride. With that in mind, my friend chose a station near where we were at the time, and after a walk of a couple hundred yards, I chose another one. I had only been in my station for a few minutes when two new cars drove in. The first, driven by a young man around 30 years old, was a sedan, and the other, driven by a very pretty young lady around the same age, was a convertible with the top down. I don't recall what makes they were, but they sure looked roadworthy. I was standing about 15 or 20 yards beyond the pumps on the edge of the highway hoping that one of them would offer me a ride, as I noticed them looking my way and talking to each other.

Alas, it was not to be. After they drove past me, waving as they drove by, the filling station attendant walked over to me and said, "You almost got a ride. One of them wanted to give you a lift so you could drive for them. The other would not agree." He didn't tell me which one wanted me to drive, and I didn't bother to ask. I didn't have to wait long after that before a four-door sedan with three ladies in it pulled up to the stop. While two of them were servicing the car, the third walked over to where I was standing and asked me where I was trying to get to. When I told her St. Louis, she asked me to remain where I was while she talked to her friends. After a short period of time, she returned and asked me to join her to talk to her friends, which I was happy to do. They all quizzed me concerning who I was, what I was doing, and my driving experience. After they held a short private conference, they asked if I would like to drive them to St. Louis, as they were continuing on east from there. Of course, I was delighted to say yes, as that put me within 125 miles of my home. They stipulated that, although they would not pay my motel fees on the trip, I would be welcome to sleep in the car if I so desired. Since I had enough money to buy my own food, this completely solved my problem, as I now also had my transportation and housing provided. As I liked to drive, the trip from there on was much more interesting, and I had a chance to see a lot of the country, which was all very scenic.

From Ogden, Utah, we angled down and hooked up with the main coast-to-coast highway connecting Salt Lake City and other major cities east. Although this was just a two-lane road, it was hard surfaced, and we made pretty good time in spite of all the twists and turns it took to get through the Rocky Mountains. Once we reached Cheyenne, Wyoming, we headed south to Colorado Springs to spend a couple of days. The three ladies I was chauffeuring (I judged to be in their mid-30s) had been on vacation together in California for a couple of weeks. Although I can't recall any of their names or whether or not they were married, they were a very jovial and happy trio and teased me unmercifully throughout the trip. Although I was 20 years of age, these young ladies in their mid-30s were much more sophisticated about life than I was and kept me blushing much of the time. However, it was all just talk, and I arrived in Colorado Springs unscathed.

Colorado Springs was a relatively small town in the 1930s, but it was one of the most beautiful towns I had ever seen. We spent a lot of time exploring the zoo and the many parks in the area, and I remember everything looked so fresh and green in contrast with the arid country through which we had been traveling. That was the only extended stop we made during the trip. So, after a couple of nights there, the decision was to head on east. The ladies had decided that they were in a hurry to get home, so the decision was made to drive nonstop from Colorado Springs to St. Louis, Missouri. That was a distance somewhat in excess of 800 miles, all of which was on narrow two-lane highways which passed through the center of every town en route.

We left Colorado Springs at daybreak, and after about 18 hours of driving time arrived in the outskirts of St. Louis. Since I had driven every mile, and even though I was in great physical condition, I was exhausted. I think the ladies felt a little guilty about this, as they had napped throughout much of the trip. So, when they dropped me off at the intersection of Highway 60, which led from St. Louis to Cape Girardeau and further south, they registered me at the motel at the intersection and paid for my night's lodging. Needless to say, I wasted no time getting settled in for my first night's sleep in a bed for 10 days or more. Next morning, after a good night's sleep, I awakened fully rested and anxious to hit the road. Although I only had 125 miles to go, I became very anxious to get there, as I knew I had many things to do in the two months or so remaining prior to returning to school.

I do not recall any of the details relative to my hitchhiking from St. Louis to Cape Girardeau, except that when I arrived in Cape, I telephoned home and my father drove up from the farm to pick me up. It was great to be home, and I spent my first few days on the farm helping my father and my brother Pete bring in the hay crop. I had never lived on this farm, as my family had moved there shortly before I went to California. By this time, my father had given up his job at the Marquette Cement Company where he ran the switch engines in the marshalling yard and had returned to mainline railroading as an engineer.

I didn't realize how much I had missed my family, so it was a great reunion for all of us, and everyone wanted to hear of my many adventures, which I was happy to tell them about, probably with many embellishments. Of course, the first thing I did after I said hello to the family was to contact my lady friend who had sworn her love for me and driven me to New Madrid at the beginning of my trip. There she had shed many tears at parting and sworn eternal love. I, of course, throughout my trip remained true to her. Well, I did think of her a couple of times. I was somewhat disappointed when she informed me that during my lengthy absence of some six or seven weeks she had started dating in order to endure the lonesome summer evenings during my absence and had fallen in love with someone else.

Brokenhearted, I happened to remember a half dozen or so of the prettier girls I knew, but had never dated, and the first one I called cured my broken heart by informing me that she had always hoped I would call sometime. During the time I was home that summer, this young lady and I had a lot of fun with other young people of our age, dancing in the various "honky-tonks" in southeast Missouri to the music of their jukeboxes.

There were many of these entertainment centers throughout the United States during this era, and the jukeboxes all contained the latest recordings of popular stars. You could play the selections of your choice for 5 cents, or six for a quarter. So, for the price of two Coca-Colas and a quarter for the nickelodeon, it didn't take many couples to have dance music playing constantly.

The next thing I had to do right away was check in with my National Guard company of assignment and make sure that I was scheduled to go with them to the summer encampments scheduled to begin within a couple of weeks. That summer, all active and reserve forces within the entire corps area were to be called to active duty for joint maneuvers, as mentioned earlier, and I wanted to be sure that I went with them.

WRESTLING

After I returned from National Guard camp, I knew I had to make up my mind concerning my senior year of college. The only thing I could think of that might provide a scholarship for me was my wrestling abilities that I had demonstrated in high school and at National Guard encampments. Research into the matter didn't take long to bring up the name of Coach Gallagher, who was then the wrestling coach at Oklahoma A&M. His team at that time was the national champions and he had served as the Olympic wrestling coach for the 1932 Olympics. Even more important to me was the fact that he had been named as the 1936 Olympic wrestling coach and was looking for talent. With that knowledge, I made the decision to visit A&M and talk to Coach Gallagher.

Accordingly, a week or so later, I was once again traveling by thumb as I had earlier that year, except I was going on a much shorter trip, as Stillwater, Oklahoma, is only a few hundred miles from Cape Girardeau. Upon arrival in Stillwater, I went immediately to the college campus and inquired as to the location of Coach Gallagher and was directed to his office in the gymnasium.

When I arrived at his office in mid-afternoon, I informed his secretary I was a college student who would like to speak to the coach. I did not tell her I wasn't an A&M student, so when she went into the coach's office, she told him a student wanted to speak to him. He told her to send me in. When I walked in his office, he was busy at his desk, so I just stood there until he looked up and asked me what I wanted. I informed him that I was looking for a school where my wrestling abilities might help me get a scholarship, as I needed certain subjects that were not available to me at my previous school. Realizing it was not a time to be bashful, I pointed out that, although my previous school did not have a wrestling team, I thought my record of no defeats in high school or in military competitions might indicate that I have some potential for the Olympic team. I pointed out that the only coaching I had ever received was in high school by a football coach who had never wrestled.

After considerable discussion and his discovery that I had brought wrestling gear with me, he suggested I get dressed and meet him in the wrestling arena where some of his current team were working out. After getting directions from his secretary, I found the dressing room and proceeded to the arena where the coach was waiting. When I arrived, the coach motioned a young man over to the ring and introduced him to me as the current collegiate welterweight champion of the United States. After loosening up, this young man and I entered the ring and on signal from the coach engaged. I soon discovered that I was wrestling someone better than anyone I had ever wrestled before. In short order, I found myself getting a little short of breath and breathing hard, as my opponent had swept my legs out from under me and had all of his body weight riding on my lower body, which was very tiring. I managed to escape before he could pin me and took him to the mat, where I seemed to have the advantage for a short time.

This went on some time with neither of us being able to pin the other, but I was suffering the most, as I was not in physical shape to wrestle at this level without additional training and conditioning. This went on for a short period, and just before I reached the point of surrender, the coach called time without either of us having a decided advantage on the other. The coach asked me to get dressed and come back to his office. After a visit to the bathroom where I regurgitated everything I had consumed during the last 24 hours, I had a quick shower and reported back to Coach Gallagher's office.

Coach Gallagher was both critical and complimentary in his critique of my performance. He stated that I wrestled too much for the upper body when I should've been going for the lower body, as that is much more tiresome for your opponent. He stated my lack of training by a qualified wrestling coach was quite evident but my strength and my ability to escape from seemingly disastrous disadvantage were quite impressive. In conclusion, he told me that if I wanted to come to A&M and train with the idea of winning a position on the 1936 Olympic wrestling team, he would see that I received a wrestling scholarship.

With that, I thanked him for seeing me and headed for home. After my return from visiting Oklahoma A&M, I only had a short period of time in which to make up my mind about further schooling. Like Southeast Missouri Teachers College, Oklahoma A&M was missing a couple of the subjects that I was interested in that would prepare me for medical school. That being the case, A&M didn't offer more in furtherance of a medical career than the school in Cape. I finally decided I would try a university that would have a wider choice of subjects. I finally decided that LSU, located at Baton Rouge, Louisiana, would be my choice. I assumed that they would have a wrestling team and would most likely offer me a scholarship, since the Olympic wrestling coach had done so. When I told my parents what I had decided, my father gave me $100 and informed me that it was for books I would require and that I have to count on a wrestling scholarship for tuition and find employment for food and other expenses.

Since this was at the very height of the Great Depression, I considered this to be quite generous and was confident that I could take care of my other requirements. Since I would have too much baggage to hitchhike with, I decided to travel by rail, as travel by rail was very cheap in those days and there was a rather direct rail line from Cape Girardeau to Baton Rouge. I remember my arrival at the Baton Rouge railway station rather well, as there was a very large group of young men waiting there. They were meeting all trains and identifying freshman that they could haze, as they were the new members of the sophomore class. I looked much younger than my age in those days, and they immediately pounced on me.

When they discovered I was a transferring senior they proved to be quite helpful when I asked for directions to the university and the athletic director's office and I proceeded directly thereto. I found the athletic director's office with no problem but also found LSU did not have a wrestling team. This, of course, meant there would be no scholarship for me, and without that, my financial situation made it impossible for me to enroll at LSU. It also dictated I should immediately head for Stillwater, Oklahoma, on the first available train, as enrollment was taking place that week at most universities and colleges. So, I dipped into my $100 reserve and bought a railway ticket from Baton Rouge to Stillwater, Oklahoma.

I don't recall how many hours it took to travel by rail from Baton Rouge to Oklahoma, but it was quite a great number, and I had a lot of time to think. While I was happy to train under Coach Gallagher, I was disappointed about the curricula available. While en route and thinking everything over, I discovered that the train I was on passed directly through Norman, Oklahoma, which was the site of the state university. I also remembered that in my previous review of schools, Oklahoma had ranked in the very top of all schools along with A&M in wrestling standings and was always in competition for national championships.

Since Olympic teams were selected on the basis of individual performances, it occurred to me that I could get the courses needed for my medical school entry and still have a chance for the Olympic team if I enrolled at Oklahoma University. With that thought in mind, I got off the train in Norman during its stop there in the early afternoon and proceeded to make a call on the director of athletics and the wrestling coach of Oklahoma University. Although I don't recall much about the athletic director, the wrestling coach was very receptive and evidently was aware that I had been offered a scholarship at A&M. He immediately offered me a scholarship and, in addition, stated he would get me a job that would provide the funds I needed for food and a place to stay. Of course, this was too good an offer for me to refuse. So, I immediately told him that I would be happy to accept.

As a result, it was only a matter of two or three days before I was fully enrolled in the courses I desired to take and found a rooming house on the edge of campus at a price I could afford and was already employed as a waiter at the leading student hangout and dining place. Although the salary I received as a waiter wasn't very high, I was permitted to eat at least one meal a day and sometimes two depending on the hours I was working. I often received good tips from some of the students, even more often from their parents when they happened to be visiting. In the rooming house where I was quartered, students were assigned two per room, and I had what turned out later to be a very lucky draw. I shared a room with a first-year law student who had served as cadet colonel of the ROTC at OU the previous year. Later that fall, he would prove to be a catalyst for probably the most important career decision I would make in my life.

When I reported to the gym for my first workout, I discovered many of the other wrestlers competing for a position on the wrestling team had arrived earlier than me and had been in training for several days. Several were involved in wrestling in the several rings provided for that purpose, while others were working with weights, climbing ropes, and hanging from the high ceiling above and exercising. It was a very large and very well-equipped facility, and two or three assistant coaches were monitoring the activities of the would-be wrestlers. When I reported to the manager of the locker room, he assigned me a locker and advised me that I was to get dressed in my gear and report to the coach in his office.

When I arrived at his office, I discovered he was in wrestling gear, and after a few words of welcome, he told me to follow him to the workout room where he told me to loosen up and then meet him at an empty ring near where we were standing. I did so and discovered he was going to wrestle with me. Since he outweighed me by some 50 or 60 pounds and knew more about wrestling than I could ever hope to learn as an amateur, I wasn't really looking forward to the next 15 or 20 minutes. It turned out I was right about that, because he really drove me to my limits. However, every time I thought he was about to pin me to the mat, he would ease up and let me escape before trying something else on me. This went on for some time, but just before I was completely exhausted, he called time. I was amazed that in his critique, although he observed that I must not have had much coaching, he found me to be very strong for my size and weight and that I seemed to be able to escape from difficult positions very well. With that he instructed me to do 100 sit-ups, work with weights for approximately 30 minutes, take four laps around a quarter-mile track adjacent to the gym, and then call it a day.

He informed me that I should report to the gym every weekday after my last class so that I could have a full workout before having to report for my evening job at the restaurant. With one exception, that became my schedule for the remainder of my time at OU. He worked out with me a few more times, but normally paired me up with someone in my weight class and I found that I had much better success against them.

About three months into the semester, I suddenly found myself without a job. My weekly pay depended upon the number of hours I had worked that week, and I was always paid in cash. One Saturday evening, as we were closing up for the night and the boss handed me my pay envelope, I discovered that he had given me credit for several hours less than I had actually worked. When I called this error to his attention, he insisted that I was wrong. However, I was positive that the mistake was his, and we had an argument. When I advised him that he would pay the money owed me or I would take it out of his hide, he paid me in full and then fired me on the spot.

I realized before I arrived at my rooming house what a stupid thing I had done. Part-time jobs in Norman, Oklahoma, were simply impossible for college students to find unless they had a senior college official looking out for them. I was too embarrassed to go to the coach and ask him to help me find another job. The fact that I might not be returning for the final semester, and certainly most likely would not be going to medical school, would not enhance his desire to assist me. Although I had saved enough money to survive for a few days, I knew that I would be facing a very serious problem in the very near future.

In discussing this problem with a classmate, who happened to be a very nice young lady, she advised me she and her sister resided in a boarding house that provided three full meals a day and that it was a large house with 20 some young female students living there. She further informed me they all ate at the same time every evening, and that washing the dishes after dinner was something that the house mother didn't like to do, as in those days it was done by hand. She volunteered to discuss my problem with the house mother and at the same time try to resolve the problem of washing the dishes.

The next day she informed me that the house mother would be happy for me to have dinner with the other students every night if I would wash and dry the dishes after dinner. Needless to say, I was delighted with this solution, and volunteered to start that day. I discovered the first day that the house served delicious dinners, family style, and although I quite often had only one full meal a day, I didn't suffer from hunger for the rest of the semester. Also, from day one on the job, I never had to wash and dry the dishes, as there was always one or more volunteer to dry dishes while I washed them.

I regret that I cannot recall the name of this young lady who made it possible for me to remain in school, as that was over 76 years ago. I do recall, however, that she and her sister liked to do nice things for fellow students, such as inviting them to be guests at their home during holiday seasons when they didn't have the time or the necessary funds to visit their own homes. They always invited equal numbers of boys and girls, and I was lucky enough in 1937 to be one of the boys invited for the Thanksgiving holidays. They provided the transportation for those who didn't have their own, and I, of course, joined them in their car when Thanksgiving rolled around.

After a few hours' drive we arrived at a very large ranch complex with hundreds of cattle and large numbers of horses on the miles of pasture we drove past. Sprinkled rather generously through many of these pastures were oil pumps, all of which seemed to be in motion. Their parents were waiting to welcome us and could not have been nicer. I can't remember all of our activities, but I do remember we did a lot of horseback riding and that there were eight of us, four boys and four girls. Having somewhat exaggerated my expertise with horses, they gave me a rather spirited animal that I enjoyed riding, with the exception of the day he stepped in a gopher hole while running at full speed. When that happened, he did a full forward flip and landed on his back with my right leg still across the saddle. He slid about 10 or 15 feet on his back with the horn of the saddle, plowing a furrow about 6 inches deep in the soil. Throughout this slide, my right leg remained under the horse. Fortunately, the saddle stayed on the horse and the horn was strong enough to support both of us throughout the slide. I had retained the reins during this event, and when the horse rapidly scrambled to his feet when we came to the end of our slide I did the same, expecting to find that he had broken his leg. It turned out that other than being somewhat shaken up, neither he nor I had received any injury during the incident. That was my first encounter with gophers. The remainder of the short holiday was enjoyable. The parents of our two student hostesses could not have been more hospitable, and the eight students were very compatible. In a seemingly very short period of time, it was necessary to say our goodbyes and head back to the university. I knew all too well that my housing and dining situation at school were not going to compare very well with the luxury provided for us at the ranch.

ARMY AIR CORPS

Although I resumed my wrestling training and attendance of all classes after the Thanksgiving holiday, it became increasingly evident to me I should be considering additional career possibilities. In conversation with my roommate, the law student, he again went to great lengths to explain to me the attractions of a military career, particularly of a military career as a pilot in the Army Air Corps.

This discussion reminded me of my last National Guard encampment, marching 22 to 30 miles per day, aircraft flying overhead with pilot scarves streaming from the cockpit and my vow to be a pilot if I ever joined the military. He assured me that pilots, after one year of active service with the Army Air Corps, were in great demand by the airline industry, which was then in its infancy. His statement that pilots could demand salaries of $200 a month or more finally convinced me, and I asked him to explain to me how to go about getting into flight training.

He was quite qualified and explained everything to me, as he had fully investigated the possibilities of his joining up before discovering that his eyesight was so poor that he could never pass the physicals required. Although I didn't know at that time what my vision measurement would reveal, I was pretty sure that I had no seeing problems. Later tests revealed that I was blessed with 20/10 vision in both eyes. Once I convinced him that I was seriously interested, he was most helpful in helping me procure the necessary forms from the office of the adjutant general of the U.S. Army and assisted me in filling them out properly. I had already procured the two letters of recommendation and a copy of my college records, which were required as attachments to my application forms. After properly packaging the application with its attachments, I mailed them to Fort Sill, Oklahoma, as instructed by Army Headquarters. I was pleasantly surprised that in a matter of two weeks or so I received a letter from Fort Sill advising me that my application was in order and that physical examinations for approved applicants would be conducted on a specific date, which I can't recall, except that it was only about three weeks after I had submitted my application.

Earlier, when I had fully made up my mind, I had with considerable trepidation informed the wrestling coach of what I was doing and the reasons necessitating my actions. Although he did express regret that I would be leaving school, he seemed to fully understand my situation and did not try to talk me out of it, as it must've been obvious to him that I really didn't have any other options. As a matter of fact, he wrote one of the two letters of recommendation that I referred to above. The other was written by the chief of police of my hometown, who was also my company commander in the National Guard. He suggested I continue my wrestling activities for the remainder of the semester, or at least until I had been fully accepted into the cadet program. I was very happy to do this, as I wanted to maintain my physical fitness for whatever the future might hold. I had finally achieved the physical fitness level required of top athletes.

Finally, the day arrived for the interviews and the physical examinations of the young men through-out the United States who had passed the initial screening required, and we lucky ones were invited to report to selected Army posts for those purposes.

Along with all other approved applicants from a five-state area in the Midwest, I was invited to report to Fort Sill, Oklahoma. Other applicants from throughout the United States were invited to selected Army posts near their homes. I don't remember how many reported to Fort Still, but there was quite a large number. The interviews and physicals were conducted in the post hospital, and my first glimpse of an Army Air Corps Officer convinced me I had found my profession. Of course, I cannot recall the officer's name, but his uniform and general appearance, in my opinion, were considerably above the norm I was accustomed to in the Army and National Guard infantry.

As all pilots did at that time, he was wearing the cavalry uniform of riding britches and the shiniest boots I had ever seen, and I could visualize myself cruising in my open cockpit aircraft with my white scarf streaming in the air behind me. The officer was a young captain, probably an early 1920s graduate of West Point, and seemed to be in charge of our schedule. The physicals we received from the doctors and their assistants were the most complete and demanding that I ever received during my 77 plus years of active and retired service with the U.S. military. I learned that even a tooth cavity could disqualify you.

After completion of our physicals, we were individually interviewed by a board of officers for a considerable period of time. Their impressions and evaluations would be included in our overall report. When the board had finished with us, we were individually released and advised we were free to go and would hear from them in the very near future concerning the results of the physical and the findings of the board. When I walked out of the door of that hospital, my eyes were still dilated and I was nearly blinded by the sunlight. Some two weeks later I was informed that I had met all requirements, except that I was not yet 21 years of age, and therefore would have to wait for the next class. After I reminded Army Headquarters I would be 21 prior to February 1938, it was agreed that I would enroll in the February class. I also learned that I was the only applicant in my group at Fort Sill to pass the physical.

Additional screenings throughout the United States were conducted later to get the number required for our class. In the early 1930s, the Air Corps conducted three classes per year for a total production of 200 to 300 pilots per year. However, the decision had been made to increase that number in 1938, and approximately 300 were desired for entry in the class beginning in February of that year. Of this number, approximately 50% would "wash out" and the remainder would be commissioned as second lieutenants in the Air Corps Reserve upon graduation from advanced flying school. The exceptions were our classmates from the West Point class of 1937, who had been commissioned some six months earlier and would go through flying school as commissioned officers. Reserve officers went through flight training as cadets.

Just a couple of weeks before the semester's end at Oklahoma University and the beginning of Christmas vacation, I received a letter directing that I report to Hot Springs, Arkansas, for my pre-induction physical in the latter part of January 1938. Needless to say, I was delighted to get the good news, as I had been learning more about the Army Air Corps every day from my roommate and everything sounded great. Also, all pressures on me concerning my future had been greatly alleviated, and I was free to enjoy the remainder of my time at OU.

I don't recall much, other than saying my goodbyes to a number of people before departing for the Christmas holidays. I do remember having a wonderful month at my home in Missouri prior to reporting for pre-induction in the U.S. Army in January 1938 and entering a new world for me, a world that I would have difficulty imagining if I hadn't had the good fortune to live in it myself.

PART 2
MILITARY SERVICE

"When man has to resort to war to resolve his affairs, he's reached about his lowest level. We're back to the cave-man days where you grab a club."

– General Seth J. McKee

FIGHTER PILOT

McKee gave this account of his early days: "My introduction to the military was in the Missouri National Guard. We wore World War I uniforms. There were only two branches of the service—Army and Navy. Other changes were the equipment and missions. We didn't have an Air Force because we didn't have planes. The Wright brothers solved that problem. Our planes had open cockpits for observation and fixed landing gear. We had sod landing fields and visual navigation. We only had three fighter groups worldwide."

He continued, "In 1938 and '39, based on student performance, I was given a fighter. Originally, I preferred an attack assignment so I could buzz trees. The lower altitude gave you a greater sense of speed. Down at Red River near Shreveport, Louisiana, back in the early thirties, the guys were flying under a bridge two feet narrower than the wingspan. So they turned her on the wing to get through. Our capabilities changed as weapons became more advanced and we changed from spotting targets for artillery to active engagement."

McKee graduated from U.S. Air Corps flight training in February 1939 at the age of 22 and afterward served several months in the 20th Pursuit Group. He then served as an operational test pilot in the newly activated Test and Show Group, where, for the next four years, he participated in testing of virtually *all* aircraft produced for the Air Corps, as well as flying the British Spitfire fighter and the Lancaster bomber. He was serving as operations officer of the 1st Pursuit Squadron at Eglin Field, Florida, and became operations officer of the Eglin Field Test Group when Japan attacked Pearl Harbor in 1941.

In early 1942, he scheduled Lt. Col. Jimmy Doolittle's B-25 Squadron training for the Tokyo Raid in coordination with aircraft testing being conducted—and his close personal relationship with Doolittle would last until Doolittle's death in 1993.

In the early spring of 1943, McKee initiated the process of organizing squadron cadres of highly experienced personnel to form combat units for assignment for assistance overseas. He would go on to serve as senior squadron commander with additional duty as deputy group commander of one of these fighter groups—the 370th—which was assigned to the 9th Air Force and proceeded to England in early January 1944. McKee named his P-38 fighter "My Gal Sal" to honor his wife Sally. He was promoted to lieutenant colonel, assigned full-time duty as deputy group commander, and became group commander six months later.

McKee's career may have been over before it hardly started. The P-38s were delivered to Andover in May of 1944. His middle son, Bill, tells this story: "Pop was cleaning a plane, removing packing, etc. and decided to try it out. As he took off, bad weather suddenly moved in and visibility dropped to zero. He thought he might have to ditch the plane and bail out. Shortly thereafter, a hole opened up in the clouds and he spotted an airstrip to land on. Upon deplaning, people rushed to him and asked what he was doing there. Pop told me he responded, 'I'm on an inspection tour!'"

McKee was a "hands-on" pilot, always leading the attack formations. He painted each P-38 with the insignia, "My Gal Sal." He had *seven*! Each time he returned from combat with his plane inoperable, he would have the next repainted to reflect the number of Sals. His exceptional exploits and heroics plus the speed of the war enabled him to become a full colonel at the age of 28, never to be duplicated again.

Young McKee had advanced up the command scale to major because of his leadership skills, hands-on approach and three to four years of experience. The vast majority of recruits were just 18 to 20 years old and in many cases just out of high school. They were eager and "gung-ho" to fight for and protect their country. They were, after all, the leading edge of the generation penned by TV correspondent Tom Brokaw as *The Greatest Generation*. They were ready for battle, or thought so at the beginning. Reality kicked in when they entered combat and after receiving letters from their brides at home announcing the birth of their first child.

With mortality looming, some of the young pilots became apprehensive of battle. Flying over enemy territory and reacting to ground-to-air and air-to-air defense took on new meaning. That's when McKee's leadership was really needed. While just a few years older than them, they respectfully called him "The Old Man." He would show them a photo of his young son, Jeff, a reminder he was also in their shoes. He would admonish them of their duty, purpose, and mission, and reassure them he would be in the lead. "Just follow me," he would say.

McKee logged more than 190 hours and flew 69 combat missions while escorting bombers into France as they attacked German defenses. His engines were shot out *nine* times. He was credited with two kills, although he sometimes mentioned he got two more, "Because I saw the bastards crash into the water!"

As the *Washington Times* reported, flying a plane riddled

with bullet holes did not rattle him. "It didn't get to me at the time—I knew I was the best fighter pilot in the war and I was pretty lucky," McKee said.

D-Day

On D-Day, 6 June 1944, Army Air Corps Lieutenant Colonel Seth McKee was a 27-year-old pilot leading a group of 40 P-38 fighter planes assigned as cover for the Normandy invasion forces. Plans were coordinated to attack but weather caused a delay in preparing for the largest seaborne invasion in history. On the evening of 5 June, officers learned troops would land on the beaches of Normandy the next day. C-47s and others were already on their way toward France. The armada consisted of 1,213 warships, 4,125 landing and assault craft, 736 ancillary craft, 864 merchant vessels, 277 mine sweepers, 2,200 bombers, and close to 200,000 naval personnel.

Germans called the P-38s "fork-tailed devils," while Allied Forces saw them as "guardian angels." As leader of the mission flying the P-38s, McKee had a close-up view of every-thing happening from the shores of England to the landing beaches in France, including an aerial view of the devastation on Omaha Beach. In describing the scene he remembered, "It was total chaos. The armada seemed to stretch from England to France. I could have walked across the ship decks and kept my feet dry across the English Channel. The line of battleships rolled back and forth through the waves as they fired at Ger-man encampments in the cliffs. They kept pouring on the salvos as bodies floated in water the color of blood. My 370th Fighter Group continued our barrage for several days, refueling back and forth from Andover. After three days when the initial battles subsided, we transferred to escort bombers into France."

As McKee looked back on the ordeal he remarked, "As tough as it was, everybody, by and large, did a good job even though more than 4,000 died that day." McKee and his group went on to conduct low-altitude support for Allied ground forces, resulting in significant battle damage on most missions.

In one battle McKee dropped a bomb of napalm which landed inside a ventilator shaft, and as he looked back, he saw Germans waving the white flag of surrender. Another time flying low, he shot all the enemy squadron. He noticed the one survivor thumbing his nose at him, so he made another pass and finished him off, too. "Those guys had mothers, fathers, brothers and sisters. I felt for them. But they were fighting for their country and I was fighting for mine," he explained.

In another, returning from a bombing raid over Germany, "Several of our planes sustained major damage," McKee reported. "One had sustained extreme damage and was on fire. I ordered the pilot to bail out. His outcome did not look good. Two months later I was at my desk when to my surprise, the pilot entered the room, saluted and announced, 'Good morning sir!' I asked him, 'Where in the hell have you been?' He responded, 'You will never believe it sir, but I landed in the front lawn of the German High Command! I finally managed to escape and here I am reporting for duty sir!'

In interviews after the war, McKee was once asked if he had any pictures of the battle. "Pictures," he responded, "I didn't have time to take any damn pictures. As I've said many times, it was total chaos over there." Later he would recognize his enemy's humanity, but he was engaged in war. "They were fighting for their country, as I was for mine," he explained.

Battle of the Bulge

The Battle of the Bulge during the winter of 1944 became the longest and bloodiest battle of the war. The bitter cold and heavy snowstorms had slowed the pace of battle around Florennes. McKee's 370th Fighter Group was snowed in and unable to fly. Brigadier General Elwood "Pete" Quesada, commander of the IX Tactical Air Command, called McKee at midnight and announced, "German tanks will hit your airfield in two hours!" Quesada further informed McKee that Bastogne was being hammered, "So the Army wants you to fly above the clouds, bomb indiscriminately and bail out." After a pause, he asked McKee, "What do you think of the plan?" McKee responded quickly, "Not much, general" and General Quesada agreed. Obviously. the pilots would have been captured or died from the fall in the thick forests and all the P-38s would have been lost, severely diminishing the Allies' air superiority.

General McKee's son, Jeff, says his father later told him of his alternative plan. "Pop was going to fight the Germans on the ground by immediately rolling all napalm barrels several hundred yards toward the oncoming tanks to create a fire barrier, line the P-38s wing tip to wing tip, and 'Blow the hell out of 'em with their cannons.'"

Neither plan happened. The orders were never given because miraculously the weather suddenly cleared and the planes began dive-bombing in patterns as the fog dispersed. They then landed, rearmed, refueled and attacked German forces and supply lines again and again. And all these attacks were coordinated by the farm boy from Missouri in his 20s.

Ultimately, the Allied air superiority stopped the German's final drive on the Western Front, but not before over 20,000 Allied troops were killed, 42,000 wounded, and 23,000 captured.

Silver Star

McKee always took the lead in battle. Weather was a problem in air combat, so there were always contingency plans for battle because they had to see what to hit. Ceiling and visibility were paramount. The plans were to hit several targets. First was the number one target. If the weather did not cooperate on the number one target, they went to number two, and if not, on to number three, and so on.

On one such occasion when McKee was on a mission, son Bill relates, "On the first target one of Pop's engines got hit and had to be feathered out of commission. Everyone in his group thought he would have to return to base or bail out. He didn't. Pop was very aware of the inexperience of his pilots. They were not trained in weather and pilotage (the ability to navigate and constantly be aware of fuel requirements.) But as leader he could do all of that for them. So, he continued the fight to targets two, three and four and then landed." He was presented the Silver Star for gallantry.

Courage is not lacking fear but learning how to control it. McKee possessed it on many occasions, always responsible for his men, the embodiment of a leader. Seth McKee proved even as a very young man he was the right guy for the right time.

In later years McKee would explain, "A mission would typically have 20 to 40 aircraft and two or three would be shot down. Only about 40% of my men completed their tours. Some were shot down or turned in their wings, unable to take the stress. If you're afraid to die, you can't be a fighter pilot in war because chances are you're not going to make it. I've killed thousands of people. I'm not happy I did, but it was my job," he concluded.

During his career, he flew 130 different types of aircraft and accumulated slightly more than 8,000 flying hours. In fact, he flew every plane the Air Force had in their arsenal between 1938 and 1973, including the British Spitfire and Lancaster Bomber. He was the first pilot to drop a bomb from a Lockheed P-38 Lightning and first to fire a 75 mm cannon and rocket bombs from airborne aircraft. He became an honorary member of the air forces of South Korea, Thailand, Republic of China, Israel, and Colombia.

In his 34-year career, McKee aided the liberation of Europe in WWII, commanded forces in Asia during Vietnam, and was on the front lines of the Cold War. He retired in 1973 as commander of NORAD, the anti-nuclear missile center in Colorado.

USAFE Skyblazers

The USAFE (United States Air Force Europe) Skyblazers, precursor to the Thunderbirds, started as an informal aerobatic team formed by three 22nd Fighter Squadron pilots from the 36th Fighter Wing at Fürstenfeldbruck Air Base, Germany, in 1949. Major Harry Evans and Lieutenants Bill and Buck Pattillo (identical twins) were returning from a routine training mission over Malta in their new Lockheed F-80B Shooting Stars when Evans decided to experiment with aerobatic maneuvers.

With Evans in the lead position and Bill on the right wing and Buck on the left, they tried several difficult formation stunts which worked well. They repeated them before reaching base at Fürstenfeldbruck. The next day they repeated them several times. They added a fourth plane to the formation with Lt. Lawrence Damewood in the slot. That was the beginning of the Air Force's aerobatic coordinated formation stunt teams. Upon being given official status they practiced for five months, adding synchronized Cuban eights (figure 8s), chandelles (180-degree turns with a climb), Immelmann turns (turn and climb to position for a steep dive in a second attack—attributed to WWI German flying ace, Max Immelmann), and rolls.

The Skyblazers made their first official appearance at RAF Gütersloh (occupied Germany) in October 1949. With formation of NATO, they continued performing throughout Europe and Northern Africa through July 1952. During those years, they performed 268 shows in 12 countries in front of an estimated ten million spectators. Evans, Damewood, and the Pattillo twins continued their distinguished, decorated careers in the USAF. With various changes in personnel and technical upgrades to aircraft, the Skyblazers continued until they were officially disbanded in January 1962.

General McKee was commanding officer during the time of the formation of the *Skyblazers*. Sally fondly remembers interacting with Major Evans and the Pattillo brothers on occasions at the officers' club at Fürstenfeldbruck. This was one of several firsts General McKee experienced and initiated as a pioneer in the development of the United States Air Force.

Japan

President Johnson elevated McKee from assistant deputy chief of staff, plans and operations for the Joint Chiefs of Staff at the Pentagon to commander, 5th Air Force, Pacific Air Forces and commander of U.S. Forces, Japan. Upon his arrival in Tokyo to assume command in Japan, he was promoted to the rank of three-star general. At that time, he was quoted as saying, "This new assignment is the greatest I've undertaken during my 28 years in the Air Force."

5th Air Force

The U.S. 5th Air Force was activated 3 Sept 1942 in Brisbane, Australia, and has never been located in the United States. It is headquartered at Yokota Air Base, Japan and is the oldest continuously serving Numbered Air Force. It has a long and storied record of accomplishments in WWII, Korea, Vietnam and generally maintaining peace in the Pacific Theater.

At the time of General McKee's command, the "Fighting Fifth" had bases in Japan and Korea. Assuming command, McKee stated, "The personnel, tactical aircraft and missiles stand alert around the clock, seven days a week, ready to mount a devastating strike against any attack." During the two years McKee commanded the force, there were more than 23,000 military personnel responsible for protective surveillance of an area larger than the continental United States.

The "Fighting Fifth" excelled in WWII and Korea in the air and supporting men on the ground. The base in Okinawa would later become a major supply center for the Vietnam War. During the Korean conflict, the 5th Air Force opened a new era in airtime aviation—F-86 Sabrejets racked up a lopsided 14.5-1 kill ratio over the MiG, destroying over 1,000 and damaging over 929 in more than 625,000 combat sorties. Thirty 5th Air Force pilots became jet aces while supporting the efforts of the men on the ground.

While maintaining and defending the peace, the "Fighting Fifth" provided a humanitarian aspect built on American values. Community programs and humanitarian activities by its units and individuals continue to play a role in the good relationships between the U.S. Air Force installations and neighboring communities.

On 20 September 1959, Typhoon Vance hit Nagoya, leaving 4,500 dead, 35,000 injured, and thousands homeless. In all, 85,000 were victims. The 5th Air Force provided parcels of food, clothing, and medical services. Similar help was provided in June of 1946, when Niigata experienced an earthquake, and on January 11, 1966, a fire obliterated a square-mile section of Misawa, leaving 5,583 homeless. For those humanitarian efforts the *Fifty News* reported 5th Air Force personnel as "A group of human beings who care what becomes of their fellow man."

STATESMAN

As McKee rose through the ranks of the Air Force, he also understood his role as an emissary of the United States. Throughout his interactions with the many representatives of foreign governments and their people, he possessed the insight to convey appreciation to them in a non-threatening way while reminding them of whom and what he represented. He was able to see the big picture and construct plans accordingly. At the same time, he never forgot lessons he learned as a young Missouri farm boy of hard work, respect for the land and appreciation of his friends and neighbors.

In one of his first proclamations as he prepared to assume command of U.S. Forces in Japan, a report in the *Japan Times* on 24 May 1966 quoted General McKee as saying that he would "Strive to promote common benefits between the U.S. and Japan through smooth consultations between the defense authorities of the two nations."

Excerpts from Speeches and Press

"Even though it has been over three years since my first visit to Japan, when my aircraft landed I had the distinct feeling that I was returning to a very familiar and pleasant place to live and work among friends. Japan and the other free nations in the Far East are exerting tremendous impact upon world affairs. The vital role being played by the government of Japan and the Japanese people in achieving progress, prosperity and peace is outstanding."

-*Kanto Plainsman* 12 August 1966

5th Air Force 24th Anniversary Speech

"Tomorrow will mark the 24th Anniversary of the 5th Air Force. On this occasion I wish to extend my personal greeting to all members of the command. The history of the 5th Air Force is a proud one. The success it has attained through the years in the never-ending fight for freedom for all peoples would not have been possible without the loyalty, dedication and efficiency displayed by you, and those who came before you.

Today, the 5th Air Force faces even greater challenges. World conditions dictate we increase our vigilance, sharpen our capability to react, and renew our dedication to the task of furthering the cause of freedom and world peace.

I am confident that in meeting today's challenges, and those of the future, you not only will maintain but even surpass the already enviable record of this command."

-The *Misawa Wing Spread* 2 September 1966

19th Anniversary of U.S. Air Force Separate Service

"Sunday, September 18, 1966, marks the 19th anniversary of the U.S. Air Force as a separate service. Looking back over the past two decades, perhaps no facet of man's endeavor has seen the rapid technological advances that have been made in aviation. Many of us in the short span of our lives have witnessed the impact these advances have had upon the military and world events. Throughout the world the Air Force has been the dominant factor in the deterrent of general war and has played a key role in defending the rights of people everywhere.

"To you—the men and women, civilian and military— who serve in Fifth Air Force, I extend special greetings in the occasion of this milestone in the Air Force's history. You can reflect with justifiable pride upon the past accomplishments of this command in fulfillment of the overall Air Force mission. At the same time, I know you will look to the future. Our mission in the Far East is a grave and responsible one. The entire world will judge how well we accomplish it. I know with your continued personal sacrifice, devotion to duty, and the belief in the freedom and human dignity of man, we will succeed."

Armed Forces Day

"This Armed Forces Day marks the 19th occasion on which the people of the United States will give special recognition to their Armed Forces. During these years, there have been periods of international tensions and conflicts which vividly proved the need for a strong defense and for the service for those who provided it. Today we are enduring a particular time of conflict and world-wide tensions and our Armed Forces daily risk their lives in the defense of world freedom.

"This makes the observance of the Armed Forces Day particularly meaningful to all of us as a reminder that there will always be a need for those who defend and protect—as long as there are those who attack and aggress.

"In this view, we can take particular pride in our daily work here as we share with the Japanese Self-Defense Forces the responsibilities of the defense of Japan."

-Tokyo, 25 December 1966

"Throughout the year in our performance of duty in

Japan, we have never lost sight of our mission to stand ready to defend the peace and to protect our Christian way of life.

"May your Christmas be joyful and may the New Year bring renewed vigor and determination to our collective effort and purpose.

"We join in extending holiday greetings to members of our sister service in Japan and all our Japanese friends and neighbors."

-Stars and Stripes - Tokyo: 25 December 1966

Christmas 1966

"Christmas is a joyous and colorful time of the year. Men, women and children of many nations and many languages join in celebrating the birth of the "Prince of Peace."

"For the members of our military forces and their families, I sincerely hope that Christmas 1966 will be as full, as warm and as joyous as any you have ever experienced. As military people you are contributing daily to the fulfillment of mankind's greatest hope ... a hope that is embodied in the spirit of Christmas itself ... Peace on Earth."

"Throughout the world, our men and women in uniform have given unselfishly of themselves of providing people of many nations the most priceless gift of all ... freedom. When freedom becomes a reality for all people, we will have achieved our goal of peace. On this Christmas Day, let us renew our dedication to the attainment of that goal."

"I wish each and your loved ones a very Merry Christmas and a full and happy New Year."

Japan/US Linked Together for Security

The role of U.S. Forces Japan with respect to mutual Japanese-American security was discussed by Lt. Gen. Seth J. McKee at an America-Japanese Society luncheon held Thursday at Tokyo Kaikan:

"Declaring that there is a need for a fuller and more widespread understanding of why Japan and the United States banded together for peace and security, I think the answer to that is clear—both want the same things—a secure peace and freedom for their people and for all other peoples who wish to grow and prosper as independent nations," McKee exclaimed.

"Of one thing we can be sure—history will be on the side of the positive thinkers as we work to achieve the national purposes of both our countries and as we meet the problems and challenges that lie ahead."

-Mainichi Daily News 27 Oct 67

Farewell Speech to Japan

In July of 1968 General McKee left his 22-month 5th Air Force command to become assistant vice chief of staff, U.S. Air Force at the Pentagon. His farewell speech in part:

"I'm justifiably proud the U.S. Air Force and 5th Air Force are more capable of performing their duties than they were when I arrived. I feel particularity gratified we have been able to enhance our outstanding relations with the government and the people of Japan."

"In saying goodbye to the military and civilian personnel of the U.S. Air Force and those in the 5th Air Force, I want each of you to know that you are a credit to your respective military services and to your country. Your contribution has been of immeasurable benefit to freedom and security in this part of the world. You have my most sincere appreciation for a job well done."

USS *PUEBLO*

The decade of the 60s was one of the most turbulent in contemporary American history. The year 1968 was especially tragic. We had barely recovered from the Korean War when we became entangled in Vietnam. On 31 January the Tet Offensive saw 85,000 North Vietnamese troops catch the American Forces by surprise, attacking over 100 cities. Our collective confidence suffered other major blows including anti-war demonstrations, the assassinations of Rev. Martin Luther King, Jr. in Memphis, Tennessee, and Senator Robert Kennedy at the Ambassador Hotel in Los Angeles, California. There were also riots in Chicago at the Democratic National Convention.

In addition, North Korean provocations included the assassination attempt on South Korea's President Park Chunghee, and the surprise seizure of the intelligence vessel USS *Pueblo*, with 83 American soldiers aboard, on 23 January 1968, which sparked one of the largest tactical air buildups in Air Force history.

The massive U.S. Air Force buildup, code named "Operation Combat Fox," found Lt. Gen. Seth J. McKee smack in the middle of a potential war. It was the "high-water mark" for McKee, the 5th Air Force commander, who would go on to become U.S. Air Force assistant vice chief of staff. As commander of the "Fighting Fifth," General McKee was the *only* operational commander to immediately take action. Throughout the tense ordeal, he remained in close coordination with his chain of command from PACAF.

From his forward headquarters at Osan Air Base, 23 miles south of Seoul, General McKee controlled all Air Force tactical air defense and reconnaissance units in the Republic of South Korea. He melded together a massive show of power from various Air Force units including F-105s from Okinawa and F-4Cs from Osan, South Korea, into a unified fighting force— ready and able to meet any rapid Communist attack.

An article in *Stars and Stripes* on 30 June 1968 described it this way: "The shrill whine of powerful jets pierced the cold skies over Korea late last January as U.S. Tactical Aircraft thundered into the Republic."

Years later, McKee gave this account: "It should never have happened. The Navy always called for air support on all classified missions to put South Korea on alert. This time they didn't. During the incident I wired everyone up the chain of command and told them if nobody stops me [No one ever did] here's what I'll do: I was going to call aircraft from one thousand miles away, refuel in Okinawa and proceed to invade. It's a good thing the weather and darkness caught up with me or as President Johnson said, 'Seth would have had to invade North Korea and possibly start World War III!'"

The U.S. maintained the USS *Pueblo* was always in international waters. The crew of 83 men were abused and tortured during their 10 months in captivity. One member of the crew was killed and his body returned to the United States when the men were released after the negotiated settlement. The massive show of military power by General McKee helped negotiations and the return of the surviving crew members. The buildup of air power in anticipation of the conflict with North Korea was aborted when the crew was repatriated. The *Pueblo* is still in North Korea and is used as a museum for anti-American purposes.

For his actions, General McKee was presented the First Order of the Sacred Treasure by the director general of the Japanese Defense Agency.

General McKee's son Bill was a senior at the United States Air Force Academy when the crisis occurred. Bill reported, "As a result of the Incident, we received extra training in the Military Code of Conduct in the event of enemy interrogation in reflection of the capture of the *Pueblo* crew." An unclassified CIA analysis concluded, in part, "The *Pueblo* material strongly demonstrates the need for clear warning language and the importance of not being overly cautious about crossing bureaucratic lines of responsibility—or 'lanes in the road.'"

At the time of the seizure of the USS *Pueblo*, young radioman 3rd Class Christine Valentine was beginning to receive communications at the tributary communications station at the Long Beach Naval Shipyard, California, home port of the *Pueblo*. The *Pueblo* was one of over 150 ships generally tied up there at any particular time. Petty Officer Valentine was a senior radioman on the shift with 10 or 12 civilians and military personnel working the desks and teletypes. The station was responsible for receiving, processing, routing and filing all communications and messages to and from command's various sources, including the carrier group and 12th Naval District in San Diego, as well as the commanding officer of the Long Beach Naval Shipyard, Rear Admiral C. Munroe Hart.

Station personnel had no idea what was occurring off the coast of North Korea. It was normal to receive 5,000 messages a day. On 28 January 1968, shortly after 4:00 p.m. PT, the crypto gear began emitting piercing alarms. "We called it screaming," Valentine said. "Obviously, somewhere in the fleet an incident had occurred involving communications security."

Without any official word from the master chief of the unit, the messages spoke for themselves that the USS *Pueblo* had been attacked and boarded. Urgency for a response to the event was paramount. "Everything we saw had been compromised," Petty Officer Valentine stated. "With only a minimum of personnel, we were responding to teletype messages as fast as they spit out of the machines, quickly glancing at the header as to routing and sending them on. The civilian watch supervisor was calling anyone off duty to come in. Normally, once routed, messages were filed. There was no time for that. The teletype copies were put into bags that eventually went out the door of the station and into the building's passageways."

"Correspondingly, as radiomen, we knew the crew of the *Pueblo* had to destroy equipment and we later learned that, in desperation, they tossed classified materials overboard during the hectic assault, hoping most would sink or float away. This was the last thing one wishes to do because of security," she said. Unfortunately, most of the classified publications and equipment were retrieved by the North Koreans.

"The effect of the *Pueblo*'s capture was mind-numbing, but everyone at the station did their job under controlled chaos," Valentine concluded. For the crew of the USS *Pueblo*, it would be 10 months before they would be returned to the United States. The 12th Naval District's radiomen were awarded the Meritorious Unit Citation by Admiral T. H. Moorer, USN, chief of naval operations. The commendation read in part:

"For meritorious service from 1 July 1967 to 31 May 1969. Foremost among the stations exemplary accomplishments were the planning and execution of communications and cryptologic support for the repatriation of *Pueblo*'s crew. Their tasks were successful without precedent for guidance, handicapped by security restrictions, and tasks with its regularly assigned duties and responsibilities."

The repatriation tasks lasted 10 months.

Commander Dickman (returning to her maiden name) served on active duty from 22 October 1966 to 8 September 1969. In 1971, she re-enlisted in the Naval Reserve, was awarded a commission as a straight-line officer in October 1980, retiring from the reserves in 1997. She resides in Cape Girardeau, Missouri.

THE EARLY YEARS

McKee Family L to R
Front Row - father, Wm F. with baby brother, Al / brother, Glen /
mother, Jeffie Olivia / brother, Wm F (Pat)
Back Row - sister, Willa Dee / sister, Arneita (Neit) / sister, Olivia
(Ebbie) / Seth / brother, Edward (Pete)

The Homestead

The Lane from house to school

Field Seth regularly plowed by the homestead

Seth Returns to the Farm

WWII

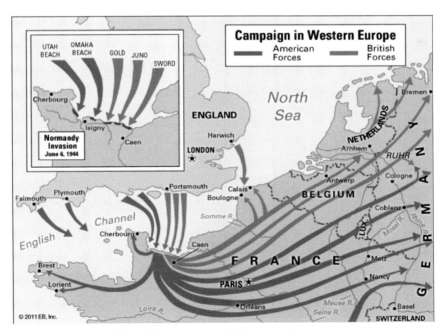

The Plan, Map of Western Europe

D-Day Map

370th to England, Troops

370th to England, P-38s

370th Group Staff

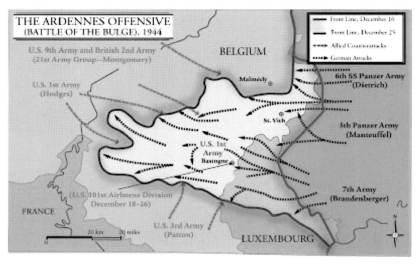

Battle of the Bulge Map

Belgium, Winter 1944

Florennes, Dec. 1944

VE Day - Paris, May 8, 1945

VE Day, Different Atmosphere

Skyblazers - "Best regards to Col. Seth McKee. We have certainly gained a lot from having served under your command and sincerely hope we may have the privilege of working for you again." ~ The "Skyblazers"

Thunderbirds

NORAD

Space Defense Center

General Danyau, Chilean Air Force, Oct. 1972

MSgt George Gary, Oath to McKee's Enlisted Aide, Aug. 1969

President Nixon Tours Cheyenne Mountain Complex, Sept. 1969

General Fourquet Chief of Staff French Armed Forces, Nov. 1969

Vice President Agnew Tours Cheyenne Mountain Complex,
Sept. 1969

Brigadier General William L. Mitchell, Jr.

Brother Pat, Sept. 1970

Tom Meyer, Arnold Roth, Cape Girardeau Businessmen, Sept. 1970

Adm. Lorenzini, Chief of Staff Italian Navy

US Senator Margaret Chase Smith & Brigadier General Tyler,
June 1972

Tennessee Ernie Ford, June 1972

Melvin Laird, Sec. of Defense, June 1972

Adm. Moorer, Chm. Joint Chiefs of Staff, June 1972

Ride with Pikes Peak Range Riders, July 1972

Mother, Talk before Dinner, July 1972

FBI Dir. Gray, Oct. 1972

Smoky 0I, July 1973

Sally McKee Certificate of Appreciation, Seth's Retirement, 1973

PRESIDENTS & AWARDS

Pres. Franklin D Roosevelt, Sept. 1934

Pres. Truman, Potsdam Conf. Stalin & Churchill, July 1945

General Dwight D. Eisenhower, Europe

Pres. John F Kennedy

Pres. Lyndon Johnson, first official White House photo
Night of the Kennedy Assassination

Pres. Richard Nixon, Sept. 1969

Receiving Legion of Honor, son Tom assisting

Legion of Honor

Legion of Honor Acceptance

General McKee Award

THE MCKEES

Bill, Tom, Sally, Seth & Jeff McKee

Sally, Miss Florida Citrus, 1940

Bill, Seth, Tom & Jeff McKee

Seth Receives 1st Star

Tom McKee

Jeff McKee

Bill McKee

Air Force Memorial

Tom's Obedient Salute!

Missouri Wall of Fame in Cape Girardeau

Mesa, Arizona Walk of Fame

50th Wedding Anniversary, 1991

THE KISS

75 Years of Marriage

... and touched the face of God.

~ excerpt from "High Flight" composed by John Gillespie Magee, Jr.

Seth as a young pilot, 1938

NORAD

On 1 August 1969, General McKee was appointed by President Richard Nixon to command the North American Air Defense Command (NORAD) located in the Cheyenne Mountain Complex near Colorado Springs, Colorado. With that appointment, he received his fourth star.

NORAD is a command deep in the solid granite Cheyenne Mountain designed to warn of a surprise attack. The United States and Canada joined forces to organize an effective defense. The buildings sit on massive steel springs designed to cushion them from earthquakes and a possible nuclear attack.

McKee commanded all strategic defense forces of the United States and Canada, comprising 300 locations throughout the world and employing more than 85,000 people. His responsibilities included air defense of the North American continent, global space surveillance and warning assessment of hostile attack from space. He had operational control of our weapons arsenal, including supersonic fighters and interceptors armed with massive rockets/missiles. He could see suspected or known enemy activity, paths of orbiting satellites, and positions of foreign submarines and ships in international waters.

Assuming the command of NORAD was one of McKee's highest achievements and he was thrilled by President Nixon's appointing him to the prestigious position. At the time, he said it was his "greatest assignment." After all, he received his fourth star and all the trappings that went with it: honor, esteem and responsibility.

"I knew and worked for all the presidents from Roosevelt to Kennedy. I didn't actually meet Truman because I was in Europe during those years. I got along with all of them. Kennedy and I clicked. When I was a major general, he even sent a Secret Service agent to personally deliver a signed photo of him to me.

General McKee retired 30 September 1973 as commander in chief, NORAD, CONAD (Continental Air Defense Commands) and ADC (Aerospace Defense Command.) However, in spite of all the trappings of his position, he was always an Airman first and fiercely protective of the Air Force. Upon his retirement, his concerns were aired to Pat Murphy, editor of *The Republic* editorial pages, in Colorado Springs, Colorado, on 27 July 1973. The article, entitled "Air Defense Chief Feels US is Vulnerable," quotes McKee as saying, "Détente with Russia has lured the United States into a Cold War euphoria which has left the nation's aging continental defenses vulnerable to a growing modernized Soviet strike force."

Before leaving as the chief of all continental defense forces in the United States and Canada, McKee reviewed America's declining military strength and evaluated Russia's growing capabilities to launch strikes anywhere in the world.

"Funding has been steadily slashed," McKee said. "NORAD's manpower has plunged from 246,720 in 1961 to 85,000 this year. Moreover, of the 504 interceptors in the NORAD force, 75 percent are operated by part-time Air National Guard units. The Semi-Automatic Ground Environment (SAGE) radar system designed to detect enemy aircraft and help guide U.S. fighters on intercept missions went into service 20 years ago."

He called his four-year tour as NORAD commander, "the most frustrating in 35 years of service." With a note of bitterness, he added, "My primary mission has been retaining what we have. The Pentagon's job has not been a division of resources, but a division of shortages. The truth is, at NORAD, we don't have adequate surveillance, we don't have adequate interceptors, we don't have adequate missiles and we don't have adequate missile defenses!"

McKee blamed the plight of NORAD and other military commands on public attitudes growing out of the Vietnam War. "Most of the public believe the military got us into Vietnam," he stated. "We didn't have a vote in that decision," he continued. "The military is one instrument of national policy and is used according to the national will."

SIX PRESIDENTS

McKee's leadership qualities and courage were apparent from his beginning days in the Army Air Corps. During his 34-year Air Force career, he held every leadership rank in the Air Force. As he rose in the ranks, his one-on-one interaction with his superiors increased. Presidents were no different.

Franklin D. Roosevelt

As a test pilot, McKee tested more than 100 different aircraft and weapons systems. He performed in air shows demonstrating the various capabilities. President Roosevelt and Canadian Prime Minister William King attended one of those air shows in Watertown, New York, in 1940.

At the conclusion, the squadron landed and lined up wing to wing. President Roosevelt's convertible stopped in front of McKee and Roosevelt motioned him to come over. McKee recalled, "After our chat, the squadron commanders wanted a debriefing as to what we discussed. It was pure happenstance, but it got me noticed."

Harry S. Truman

McKee never met or discussed issues with President Truman because he was in Europe during most of Truman's presidency. He mentioned from time to time he would have liked to have met him since they were both from Missouri.

Dwight D. Eisenhower

General Dwight D. Eisenhower was supreme commander of Allied Expeditionary Forces in Europe. He supervised the invasion of France and Germany in 1944-45. (And, of course, McKee was the group commander of P-38s, which he led up and down the coast of Normandy supporting the landing on D-Day.)

McKee recalled a meeting with Eisenhower including pilots with higher rankings than him, where Eisenhower questioned each man. "Afterwards, he turned to me and told me to stay in the room. He then told the others to leave, saying, 'This man is the only one who gave me the strategic information I needed.'" Through the years, McKee would occasionally remark, "I Liked Ike!"

John F. Kennedy

"President Kennedy and I clicked. He was a great man," McKee exclaimed. "We saw eye to eye on many issues, probably because we were of the same general age. When I was a major general, he even sent a Secret Service agent to personally deliver a signed photo of him to me. He was a good listener, unlike several of his young, close advisors. He once told me he had special plans for me. But of course, Lee Harvey Oswald ended that. Kennedy and Johnson didn't get along too well. Kennedy never let Johnson off the plane until he had greeted all the dignitaries.

Lyndon Johnson

"Lyndon Johnson was an odd fish but we got along. I

knew him from his Senate days. After I testified before his committee one day, he wrapped his arm around my shoulder as we walked down the hall and said, 'General, you're doing a great job.'"

Richard M. Nixon

In 1969, President Nixon became the first president to visit the NORAD underground command post. By that time, General McKee had been elevated to command the site by President Nixon. McKee briefed the president and members of his party on his ability to observe any known or suspected enemy activity including positions of foreign and orbiting satellites and hostile submarines or ships in international waters. Guests included Secretary of State Dr. Henry Kissinger, Attorney General John Mitchell, and several U.S. Senators.

McKee recalled, "At NORAD I was over the U.S. and Canada. There was no one between me and the President during Nixon's terms on the nuclear button. As I was explaining the chain of command to Nixon, which was from president to vice-president to speaker of the house, and then to me, Nixon stopped me: 'No, No, No' Nixon exclaimed, 'If you can't find me, you're the boss. Don't consult the vice-president [Spiro Agnew] or anyone else. You're in charge—*you* do it!'"

REFLECTIONS

Character

"I learned hard work and moral ethics on the farm. Cultivating 25 acres with one plow and a pair of mules for several weeks taught you to finish the job." On more than one occasion he remarked, "School was easy compared to plowing a field. I was never hungry growing up on the farm. We had plenty to eat. But everyone was poor in rural Missouri; it was during the Great Depression. I liked to do everything better, and I like to think I did."

Responsibility

"Regardless of the level of responsibility that you hold through life, if you make every effort to be the best among your peers at that level, your superiors will take notice and appropriately move you up the ladder to the next higher level on an accelerated schedule. If you have the capability to do that at every level you achieve in life, you will eventually end up among those at the top."

Commands

"I always operated under the tenet that I would carry out orders given unless they were detrimental to the United States. My job was to protect the country at all costs—to the last man if necessary. Under those circumstances, I would give my opinion, and if the order stood, I would resign. Thank God I never had to," he remarked. "When asked if I was satisfied with my decisions, I always replied, 'I would always like to do better, but I did the best under the circumstances … no Monday morning quarterbacking.'"

Leadership

"Sally believes my leadership qualities of honesty, concern for my men, ability to perform under stress, clear thinking, void of strain and tension during war were grace from God. A bit much, don't you think? My challenge was to keep the peace. Unfortunately, sometimes we had to go to war to accomplish it. And defend to the last man if necessary. The worst part was losing so many good, young, talented men and women. But I make no apology for it," he concluded.

Military Wives

"Military wives are very important and my Sally was the best. She was comfortable with kings, queens, emperors, and just plain folks. Wives can't promote an officer but they can make or break one. Once in a while, an officer's wife would think the others should follow her lead. I operated under the premise that all wives were equal, and had no power unless they were in uniform. Military wives sacrificed plenty keeping the home fires burning and raising the family. Their support was crucial," he said admiringly.

World Affairs

"We are not trained to be the world's police force. Every country has different values, thinks differently. But we spend *billions* trying to make them in our image. If anyone was foolish enough to launch a nuclear attack, the other would have to respond. Everyone would have too much to lose. Most countries have a good life compared to their past."

Japan

"Everything went through me in Japan. I held the command General McArthur did 10 years earlier. I was with Emperor Hirohito three or four times a year. He wanted to know that his country was secure. I said it was and I expected the same from him! I always tried to be civil and understanding of their culture and accepted them for whom and what they were. The wives of their military treated Sally royally. I met our ambassador and the commanders of our Army and Navy once a month to promote teamwork. We would generally play a round of golf and finish with dinner," he explained.

Vietnam

"It never should have happened," McKee exclaimed. "We had a group called the Little Chiefs of Staff that met weekly. President Kennedy had prepared to bring all of the troops home by Christmas. Soon after Kennedy was assassinated, at a key meeting, the chief of staff of the Army presented us the proposal to raise troop levels from 10-15,000 so-called advisors to 50,000. I asked why. He said, 'To better protect your air bases.' I replied, 'You already do a good job. We don't need more protection. If you bring that many you'll have too many men at base. And furthermore, you'll have to set up a 10,000-mile pipeline to support those troops.' He insisted. I was a major general and he was a four-star general—end of story," McKee explained.

Russia

"We were always leery of Russia, always watching them. We had a B-52 with nuclear weapons regularly circling the North Pole. I never believed there would be a nuclear war. Most countries would have too much to lose. They have developed their societies to the point that their lives are fairly good and they would have to be willing to lose something they already have. And, they would have to be prepared to absorb all our weapons or end the world as we know it," he warned.

McKee's Greatest Day—VE Day

"I was commander of a P-51 group in Northern Germany at Fürstenfeldbruck, the old German Headquarters we had captured, and I'd returned to Paris after a short leave prepared to go back to battle. We awoke to horns blasting, whistles blowing and thousands of people marching in the streets. I asked the closest person, 'What the hell is going on?' He replied, 'The Germans have surrendered, *the war is over*!' I spotted an army major and commandeered his jeep and had him drive us so we could join the celebration on the Champ-Elysees and drink some of the free-flowing champagne. I may have been the only colonel in the parade," McKee proudly stated. "It was reported that the plane that buzzed the Arc de Triomphe was a P-51. And I thought, *Oh My God, I hope it wasn't one of mine or Eisenhower will fire me.* It was, but nobody ever mentioned it," McKee reported thankfully.

McKee Says Gulf Conflict Same as WWII

During his visit to Cape Girardeau in January 1991, General McKee explained to *Southeast Missourian* staff writer Jay Eastlick that the Persian Gulf war was different than previous conflicts in Korea and Vietnam. Operation Desert Storm was more like World War II. U.S. airstrikes against Iraqi troops in

Kuwait and Iraq compare to massive bombing missions against German forces in Europe. During the first week of Operation Desert Storm, more than 10,000 bombing missions were flown in Kuwait and Iraq. In WWII up to 2,000 fighter planes flew continually against German forces. Although fighters of today carry more firepower, the fighter bomber business is still the same. Machine-gun 'dog-fights' have given away to 'air-to-air' missile combat between high-powered jet aircraft. My P-38 shared the same mission as the F-15E Eagle, F-117 Stealth and Navy A-6. Our accuracy was largely determined by the pilot and crew. Today it's determined by the effectiveness of electronics and computer systems.

Smart weapons have helped to reduce civilian casualties because of much more precise accuracy. That accuracy enables us to only destroy our military targets and our enemy's defense capabilities. The U.S. Patriot surface-to-air missiles we worked to develop at NORAD in the middle 1970s seems to be performing very well. They should continue those air strikes. It appears we have learned some lessons from Vietnam by allowing the military to use its best efforts in conducting the war instead of politicians and Washington bureaucrats.

MILITARY AWARDS and DECORATIONS

Chevalier de la Légion d'Honneur (2016)

In 2016, at the age of 100, General McKee was awarded the rank of Chevalier (Knight) by the Republic of France for his leadership in the liberation of France as a commanding officer during WWII. The award is from the National Order of the Legion of Honor, the highest award France bestows on its citizens and foreign nationals.

Because of McKee's rank and age, the French government sent Brigadier General Vincent Cousin, the defense attaché from the French Embassy in Washington, to make the presentation. In part, General Cousin remarked, "The young recruits from America were instrumental in supporting French soldiers and civilians worn out by five years of fighting and occupation. The Allied Landings and air support in Normandy were decisive in ending Germany's occupation of Europe."

General McKee surprised his family and friends by spritely rising from his wheelchair as General Cousin pinned the Legion of Honor Medal to his lapel. McKee thanked the French

Government for their friendship to the United States throughout history and quipped, "I've been honored by the French before, but the last time, General de Gaulle kissed me on both cheeks."

The Legion of Honor was established in the 1800s by Napoleon to honor those who displayed distinguished valor and significance to France. The first foreign nationals to receive the award were those who fought on French soil in WWI from 1918 to 1919.

Gerrit Steenblik is an attorney in Phoenix and was honorary consul for the French government in charge of finding WWII U.S. veterans who qualified for the Legion of Honor in Arizona between 1999 and 2018. He contacted his friend, Dewey Schade, who he thought might know of someone who could qualify. Schade introduced him to General McKee, a major contributor to the liberation of France. While Steenblik usually presented the commendation in the name of the President of the Republic, he coordinated McKee's event.

"The French people still have a love affair with the Allies including the Brits, Canadians, and Australians who gave their lives in defense of the homeland. They have never forgotten their actions that ultimately turned the tide," Steenblik remarked. His family returned to France for the 75th anniversary of D-Day. "It was inspiring to see people demonstrating everywhere with American flags, and hundreds of restored vehicles up and down the streets, in towns and small villages, cafés, restaurants and hotels. It reminded us of the reservoir of cooperation that still exists between the U.S. and France, especially at the operational level of sharing intelligence and strategies to fulfill military missions," he said.

Distinguished Service Medal

Silver Star

Legion of Merit with two oak leaf clusters

Air Medal with 10 oak leaf clusters

Croix de Guerre with Palm (France)

Croix de Guerre with Palm (Belgium)

Belgium Fourragere

Order of Leopold with Palm (Belgium)

First Class Order Royal Crown (Thailand)

Order of Sacred Treasure

First Class (Japan)

National Security Merit

Second Class (Republic of Korea)

Distinguished Flying Cross
> *"for extraordinary achievement while participating in combat operations against the enemy in the European Theater"*

Air Medal with 10 oak leaf clusters

Croix de Guerre with Palm (France)

Croix de Guerre with Palm (Belgium)

Order of Leopold with Palm (Belgium)

First Class Order Royal Crown (Thailand)

Order of Sacred Treasure (Japan)

First Class (Japan)

Order of National Security Merit (Republic of Korea)

Second Class (Republic of Korea)

THE GENERAL SETH J. MCKEE AWARD

The General Seth J McKee Award is one of the most coveted awards for AFSPC's best space warning system. Upon General McKee's retirement in 1973 after a distinguished 37-year career in the United States Air Force, the award was established in his honor. The award is presented annually to the best missile warning squadron, both space-based and ground-based, in the 14th Air Force and Air Force Space Command for the most significant contributions in support of the overall space mission. Primary criteria for the award encompass mission accomplished, meritorious achievement, quality of life and safety, and community service.

Recipients

1975   14th Missile Warning Squadron
1976   2nd Communications Squadron
1977   20th Surveillance Squadron
1978   Space Defense Center

1979	5th Defense Space Communications Squadron
1983	5th Defense Space Communications Squadron
1984	5th Defense Space Communications Squadron
1985	2nd Communications Squadron
1986	PAVE PAWS –7th Missile Warning Squadron & 2156th Communications Squadron
1987	4th Satellite Communications Squadron
1988	5th Defense Space Communications Squadron
1989	10th Missile Warning Squadron
1990	10th Missile Warning Squadron
1991	20th Communications Squadron
1992	4th Space Warning Squadron
1993	2nd Space Warning Squadron
1995	2nd Space Warning Squadron
1996	11th Space Warning Squadron
1997	3rd Space Control Squadron
1998	11th Space Warning Squadron
1999	11th Space Warning Squadron
2000	2nd Space Warning Squadron
2001	7th Space Warning Squadron
2002	2nd Space Warning Squadron
2003	7th Space Warning Squadron
2004	2nd Space Warning Squadron
2005	7th Space Warning Squadron
2006	13th & 213th Space Warning Squadrons
2007	2nd Space Warning Squadron
2008	10th Space Warning Squadron
2009	11th Space Warning Squadron
2010	2nd & 8th Space Warning Squadrons
2013	460th Operations Group Det 1
2015	460th Operations Group Det 1
2016	2nd Space Warning Squadron

PART 3
THE AMAZING
MCKEEs

"My proudest accomplishments were as husband, father, grandfather and great-grandfather."

– General Seth J. McKee

FAMILY TIME

My Gal Sal

It is impossible to tell General McKee's story without including his amazing family, beginning with his marriage to the remarkable Sally Parshall. They were united in marriage on 7 June 1941, in Orlando, Florida. Seth was from Missouri and with one of the first units to train at the old Orlando Air Base. Sally was a member of one of the area's pioneer families and the reigning Miss Florida Citrus. The wedding was one of the social highlights of that pre-war era, and included 12 bridesmaids and 12 groomsmen. The Associated Press estimated the crowd to be 4,000.

McKee recalled meeting her when the city of Orlando had a welcoming dance for the airmen and officers of the Air Corps, which opened its Orlando base in August of 1940. "I thought she was the prettiest girl I'd ever seen," recalled McKee. "I instantly knew she was the gal for me, but it took her a little longer," he chuckled. (Years later when asked about his analysis, Sally quipped, "Not Really!") "Needless to say, everyone wanted to dance with her so I was cut in on about every three dance steps. This went on all evening," McKee remembered.

Sally had just returned from a goodwill trip to the New York City Stork Club, where she made an appearance on stage to present a bushel of oranges to Glenn Miller and his Orchestra. "He surprised me when he even asked me to sing," Sally remembered. "While I did sing at times, I wasn't a professional, so I declined. I was in New York for about a week. Actor Paul Douglas was my escort as I passed out oranges everywhere we went. I attended the Broadway Show *Hellzapoppin* and met Olsen & Johnson, the great comedians and stars of the show. I heard Fred Waring and His Pennsylvanians at the famed Café Rouge in the Hotel Pennsylvania, the hotbed of the big bands in those years. It was a wonderful trip," she fondly remembered.

Seth and Sally were married the day after Sally graduated from high school. As she was walking in the graduation procession, her escort, who had a crush on her, remarked, "This won't be as grand as tomorrow." Sally's explanation was, "I was 16 and Seth was a dashing young second lieutenant at age 24. Up to then I had only dated boys my age or an occasional college boy when visiting the Citadel and Florida State University as college possibilities. I never had a crush on anyone, let alone ever been in love." Sally continued, "My mother loved Seth. My father had passed away and Seth kept saying, 'Your dad would have liked me and approved of our marriage.' Mom agreed."

In today's world, with the glitter and trappings of high command, they would have been seen by many as "rock stars." But they were serious and down to earth with military personnel and civilians and produced one of our country's most honored military families.

Throughout their careers, General McKee and Sally were a team. Sally always supported the troops as the wife of an officer, and as a "Gray Lady" with the American Red Cross. Their partnership played an important role for morale of the troops. It was not uncommon for them to take separate itineraries when touring facilities. On tour of the Yokota Air Base, the general visited the 35th Tactical Fighter Squadron hanger, the 441st Field Maintenance Squadron engine room on the flight line, the 441st Supply Squadron, commissary, non-commissioned officers open mess, and the airman barracks. Sally's schedule took her to the base nursery, the Falcon Service Club, the Red Cross office, the base chapel and the 6034th dispensary.

They made quite a striking couple receiving dignitaries, hosting formal military receptions, parties, community programs, humanitarian events, and more as demanded by the various ranks of McKee's appointments. Those events were attended by small groups and as many as a thousand or more. McKee always said Sally was the best. "She was the epitome of grace and elegance. She was equally at home with civilians, diplomats, career military personnel, generals, statesmen, rulers, even presidents. And she was pretty good with a pool cue stick."

The McKees were proud of their family. "As serious and proud as Seth was of his military service, he was first and foremost a family man," Sally said. "We had a very good loving relationship. After all, we survived *thirty-two* moves! Our boys came approximately three years apart; Jeff in 1942, Bill in early 1946, and Tom in 1948. They were good little troopers. They generally adapted well to the constant upheaval of leaving friends and schools every couple of years to move on to Seth's next assignment." She remembered, "On one occasion when we were transferred from Homestead Air Force Base near Miami, Florida, to Omaha, Nebraska, we wouldn't get there until after high school started. General Jack Ryan, who would become chief of staff of the Air Force, took Jeff, who was 16 at the time, to live with his family until we arrived a month later. General Ryan even tutored Jeff at night. Another time Bill stayed with his best buddy until school started."

The McKee family was closely knit. Sally managed

to juggle her official duties while raising three boys. McKee remarked many times, "My proudest accomplishments were as husband, father, grandfather, and great-grandfather." He was also known to remark occasionally with the ever-present glint in his eye, "I always liked to be in command, in control. I generally found it to be present everywhere except in my *marriage*." The McKees were married for 75 years and have three sons, eight grandchildren, and nine great-grandchildren.

Lt. Col. Seth J. (Jeff) McKee, Jr., USMC-USAF

JEFF MCKEE was born in 1942 in Orlando, Florida, the oldest of the three sons. Jeff spent time with his younger brothers while on weekend family outings camping and boating, going on vacations, and attending church. Each day the family would eat dinner together, where everyone's daily events would be discussed. On occasion, the boys' commitment to each other would be reinforced as they stood up to bullies at each new duty station. As the years passed, Jeff's activities gradually took him away, except from family functions, holidays, and other special events.

Jeff had become bored with college at Creighton University during his second year when he entered the student union for lunch. "It was happenstance," he remembered. "The man sitting next to me was a marine recruiter." As they talked, the recruiter told him the marines were offering a Marine Aviation Cadet (MarCad) flight training program for young men who wanted to fly. It consisted of two years of college and passing the necessary tests and physicals.

"I always wanted to fly so I signed up. I didn't tell Pop I had enlisted in the Marine Corps rather than the Air Force until I announced it to a room full of relatives who were visiting us at home," Jeff remembered. "Pop was always supportive of me and he swore me in as a United States Marine in 1963." That decision led to a distinguished 39-year career in aviation as a decorated TOPGUN fighter pilot in the Marine Corps with tours in Vietnam, a captain for TWA and American Airlines, and a lieutenant colonel in the California Air National Guard.

"Flying always came easy to me," Jeff said. He received extensive training at the Naval Air Station Pensacola, Florida, for indoctrination and preflight training, then on to Saufley Field for primary flight training where flight grades determined whether you went to the jet or helicopter pipeline. Jeff went into jets and thus to Naval Air Station Meridian for basic jet training and acrobatic flight, then onto VT-21 training squadron for air carrier landings, and finally to Kingsville, Texas, for advanced jet training graduating as a second lieutenant.

His first duty assignment was in Beaufort, South Carolina, with VMF(AW)-235 fighter squadron for six months more training, then to Da Nang, Vietnam Marine Air Group 2 for two tours, flying 150 missions and serving with 3rd Battalion, 9th Marines as forward air controller (in the jungle) where he directed air strikes. He received the DFC, a Presidential Citation for Distinguished Airmanship in Protection of U.S. Forces in Hostile Territory. He flew the F-8 Crusader in Vietnam, the F-102, the F-4 Phantom in the Air National Guard, and every plane at TWA except the 747. His duties in Beaufort included being a fighter operations officer, test pilot, and instructor pilot.

Jeff's military awards and commendations include the Distinguished Flying Cross, Bronze Star with Combat V, seven Air Medals, the Purple Heart, Navy Unit Commendation, and associated campaign medals.

In his retirement, Jeff has worked on projects for his church and Habitat for Humanity. He holds memberships in MENSA, the Experimental Aircraft Association (he built and flew his own aircraft from California to St. Louis), and Aircraft Owners and Pilots Association. He enjoys golf, scuba diving, camping, and is an accomplished sculptor and artist.

Jeff was always interested in art. "I tried to keep my interest in art a secret at school," he explained. "Teachers wanted me to stay after school to complete projects when I always wanted to be outside with all the other kids. As a result, my passion for art lay rather dormant. On the occasion of Mom and Pop's 50th anniversary, the boys thought it would be appropriate if I would construct something unique we could present to them. So I cut down a walnut tree in my yard and made an abstract child from the numbers 5 and 0."

That experience got Jeff's creative juices flowing, so he also began sculpting in stone, bronze and other materials in his home studio. In addition, he took up painting. Jeff's works can be found in many public buildings, private homes, corporate headquarters, and galleries around the country.

Even with all that, Jeff was bored, so he became a private investigator! He is a member of the American Association of Private Investigators, working for major companies and individual clients out of his home in Kirkwood, Missouri, where he lives with his wife, Virginia. He has two sons, Seth III and West, and a daughter, Dorian.

Capt. William B. McKee, USAF

BILL MCKEE was born in Orlando, Florida, in 1946. He graduated from Creighton Preparatory School in 1964, remaining at Offutt Air Force Base for six months after his father was reassigned as commander 821st Air Division at Ellsworth Air Force Base, South Dakota. He is a distinguished graduate of the United States Air Force Academy (1968), winning both presidential and congressional nominations. He earned a master's degree in economics from UCLA in 1969.

His military service included being an advanced instructor pilot in T-38s at Laughlin Air Force Base, Texas, and a PIT instructor to train instructors and requalify returning POWs from Vietnam at Randolph Air Force Base, Texas. He later flew the F-106 Delta Dart as an interceptor pilot for the Air National

Guard in New Jersey.

Bill and his wife Penne moved to Phoenix, Arizona, in 1974, where he completed a civilian career in corporate finance including venture capital, commercial, and investment banking, and serving on many public and private boards. After leaving the Air Force, he remained an active aircraft owner/pilot, operating various twin-engine aircraft up to and including the Cessna Citation.

He retired in 2000 and graduated from Fuller Seminary in 2015, where he earned a master's degree in theology. He is currently Scholar in Residence at Valley Presbyterian Church in Paradise Valley, Arizona. Bill has published a book on theology and teaches adult education. He and Penne have two children, Sarah and Bob, and two grandchildren. They live 30 minutes from his mother, Sally, and tend to her extended needs. At this writing (2020), Sally is in good health, bright, and an alert 95 years young.

Capt. Thomas J. McKee, USAF

TOM MCKEE was born 23 October 1948 in Montgomery, Alabama, the youngest of Seth and Sally's three sons. He attended first and second grade at Williston Elementary with Jeff and Bill in Falls Church, Virginia. "The longest we stayed anywhere was in Omaha, Nebraska, from 1959 to 1964. I attended Creighton Prep High School in Omaha, but soon transferred to Douglas High School near Rapid City, South Dakota, when Pop was made Division Commander at Ellsworth Air Force Base. Following a year at Ellsworth, we went back to DC, where Pop arranged for us to live on the top floor of Prospect House which still provides the best view of DC, staring right down the Mall. I graduated there from Washington-Lee High School in 1966. Pop went to Japan to be Commander, US Forces Japan and 5th Air Force and I went to Cape Girardeau to start my first year at Southeast Missouri State University," Tom remembered.

Tom earned a Bachelor of Arts degree in political science from Southeast Missouri State University in Cape Girardeau, Missouri in 1970 (the same institution his father attended). He joined the Sigma Chi Fraternity where he became the chapter president. Later in his career, he was recognized as a "Significant Sig" from the International Fraternity. Following college, he was commissioned in the United States Air Force through Officer Training School at Lackland Air Force Base, Texas, and completed undergraduate pilot training at Reese Air Force Base, Texas, in October 1971. During his active service, Tom performed duties as a T-38 instructor pilot/check pilot and flew the A-7D Corsair II while assigned to the 356th Tactical Fighter Squadron at Myrtle Beach Air Force Base, South Carolina.

In March 1977, Tom separated from the Air Force and joined the Grumman Aerospace Corporation in Bethpage, New York. In 1988, he was transferred to Grumman's Washington operations and was elected a corporate vice-president by the board of directors. He is past chairman of the board and national president of the Air Force Association, and one of the six founding charter trustees of the Air Force Memorial Foundation. As a result of his distinguished civilian service to the United States Air Force, he was presented the Exceptional Service Award by the Secretary of the Air Force in 2000. He also served as a trustee on the Falcon Foundation at the United States Air Force Academy in Colorado Springs; and for over 30 years as a trustee of Vaughn College of Aeronautics and Technology in New York City, seven of those years as chairman of the board.

Tom and his wife, Patricia, have two daughters and one son, Michelle, Catherine and Tom, Jr., and seven grandchildren. They currently live in Fairfax Station, Virginia, near all of their children and grandchildren.

Air Force Memorial
"The United States Air Force has been my life, having

167

grown up in a decorated Air Force family," proudly states Tom McKee. "Following the 1990 Gulf War, I was humbled when asked by Oliver R. 'Ollie' Crawford, national president of the Air Force Association, to join him and the great World War II Ace and Flying Tiger, Major General John Alison, along with Jack Price of Utah, Marty Harris of Florida, and George Douglas of Colorado to serve as one of the six founding charter trustees of the Air Force Memorial Foundation." The Foundation's purpose is to honor the men and women of the United States Air Force and its heritage organizations and was incorporated in 1992.

Groundbreaking commenced in September of 2004, and construction was completed in two years, followed by the dedication attended by 30,000 people on 14 October 2006. President George W. Bush, a former F-102 Delta Dagger pilot with the Texas Air National Guard, gave the address which included in part:

"To all who have climbed sunward and chased the shouting wind, America stops to say: your service and sacrifice will be remembered forever."

The memorial sits atop a promontory overlooking Arlington National Cemetery near the Pentagon. The three stainless steel spires soar 201, 231 and 270 feet respectively, reaching 402 feet above sea level. The grounds also include inscription walls, a bronze Honor Guard statue, parade ground, ceremonial pathways, and a Glass Contemplation Wall depicting the "missing man" flying formation.

"The honor to be one of the six original founding trustees allowed me to continue my service to the greatest Air Force in the world," Tom exclaimed. The memorial means different things to different people. "My two brothers and I can relate to the three spires flying a bomb burst around the star symbolizing our respect and gratitude for the sacrifices Pop and our mother made throughout their Air Force career and during his service in

World War II."

Our Dog, Raider

"Raider was a large boxer. He had one ear that flopped down and the other stood up like it should," oldest son Jeff described. "He originally belonged to someone else in Frankfurt, Germany. He used to come running at us as we played, so we gave him the name *Raider*, as he was always raiding us. When the people got transferred, they gave him to us. Raider lived in our backyard in Fürstenfeldbruck, Germany. He would catch hedgehogs, rabbits, everything. He would fight other dogs, so we always had to keep him penned up. Every once in a while he would get out so I would chase him before he would fight the other dogs."

Bill chimed in, "We were constantly looking for him when he got out of the backyard. We'd go all around the neighborhood yelling 'Raider, Raider!' He liked to go up to Glebe Road where he would chase cars, trying to bite their hubcaps."

Jeff laughed as he told this story: "One time, Raider was gone for an unusually long time. Our house was off the base. We saw him coming back across the field dragging a dead pig with a farmer following with a shotgun. Pop paid for the pig!"

When they returned to Washington, DC, from Germany, Jeff helped Seth build a fence in the backyard for Raider. "One day, he somehow got out," Jeff said. "As I chased him, he ran across a highway and got hit by a car. I carried him all the way home and laid him in the front yard. About that time, Pop came home from the Pentagon on crutches with a foot injury from playing basketball during lunch. He said no one paid any attention to him on crutches because they were huddled around Raider wondering if he was going to live or die. He lived."

According to Sally, "We all liked Raider. Seth had a large red leather chair and he liked to jump up in Seth's lap. Raider was Seth's lap dog," she said as she chuckled. "Seth walked him every evening. Seth was a family man. He loved the boys," Sally said. "He was the leader of their Boy Scout Troop in DC, president of their elementary school PTA and camped and fished with them on the weekends."

Jeff said in spite of all the gambits, "Raider was a good and loyal dog. When we moved to Savannah, Georgia, Pop said he gave him to a farmer so he could have a lot of room to run and play. I guess he was telling us the truth," Jeff surmised.

Being the youngest, Tom doesn't remember much about the early years of Jeff and Bill. "Pop was a full colonel during the years from 1948 through 1959," Tom explained. "As a kid, I only remember him as a senior officer. He was still the youngest colonel at the end of the war and we were still on the move throughout those years."

He does remember a story his mother told when his dad was an attaché in Rome, Italy. "Mom hired a governess to tutor me," Tom explained. "The governess called me *Little Bambino*. She was teaching me Italian, so I was speaking mostly Italian. Mom fired her because she couldn't understand what I was saying."

Tom continued, "I attended first and second grade at Williston Elementary School along with Jeff and Bill when we were in Falls Church, Virginia. I'd ride my bicycle around the neighborhood. One of our favorite places was an empty lot with a network of holes and tunnels. We'd sit in the holes thinking no one knew where we were in our own little world. Pop surprised us one late afternoon when he stuck his head into the tunnel and said dinner's ready. He evidently knew where we were all the time."

Hunting and Fishing

Sally said, "The family did a lot of boating on the weekends. At one point, a bunch of officers all bought outboard motorboats." Seth and Sally joined the group with 15-year-old

Jeff as "captain" of their boat. "We called ourselves 'the Squadron.' The Squadron fished, camped, water-skied, and one week all boated to the Florida Keys and back."

"Pop's relatives were campers," Tom said. "When we went back to Scott City, Missouri, we always camped. One of our favorite spots was on the Eleven Point River fed by springs in the beautiful, pristine Ozark National Scenic Riverways. It was great for hunting, fishing, and canoeing. Those rivers are wild and swift with deep eddies and sharp turns. Our Uncle Pete was a true outdoorsman very familiar with those rivers and adept at handling a boat. We always felt safe with him at the helm. On one trip when I was about 11 years old, the current was exceptionally swift. Uncle Pete took a left turn too late and we slid about 30% up a tree that had leaned into the river. We capsized. Mom grabbed my wrist tightly and held me up as she went under. We all survived, but Uncle Pete lost his large prized tackle box along with his keys, wallet, watch and more. Two years later, a fisherman found his tackle box downstream and returned all the belongings to Uncle Pete."

Counsel

In their early years, the boys would ask questions of their dad about his job and things they would hear at school. Once Jeff heard the Apollo 8 astronauts paid his dad a visit at the Cheyenne Mountain Complex, had dinner, discussed the flight, and showed him some moon rocks. "Mom didn't remember, which wasn't surprising," Jeff said. "Most of Pop's duties were classified and he couldn't talk about them – so growing up we finally just quit asking.

"Even though Pop was an Air Force man, he always supported me when I entered the Marine Corps." Jeff explained. "On one occasion during Vietnam, I surprised him when I flew an F-8 Crusader back to Osan that had been shot up. I had to ferry it to Atsugi, Japan. I was restricted to Mach .78 due to battle damage it got while I was flying it on a mission." Jeff continued, "During my brief stop, Pop was to give a speech on the Air Force that night at a dinner. He invited me to go along. The only clothes I had was my uniform. All the people in attendance were in civilian clothes. He surprised me by changing the topic and giving an impromptu talk on the Marine Corps!"

In discussing where Tom was to go to college, Seth said, "Why don't you try Southeast Missouri State College in Cape Girardeau where I went? You've got family there, it's a good school, and after a couple of years, if you want, you can transfer to a bigger school." Well, no one knew at the time how fortuitous that decision would be, especially Tom.

One day, sitting in Myers Hall, his roommate asked, "Do you want to see Miss New Jersey?" Looking out the window Tom saw a tan coed in a tight red skirt and white blouse and exclaimed, "She's gorgeous!" (Similar to Seth's reaction to seeing Sally for the first time many years before.)

As fate would have it, Patricia wanted to be an elementary teacher and her high school counselor had recommended Southeast because of its reputation as an outstanding teacher education school. They spent many hours together as Patricia became President of Alpha Chi Omega sorority and Tom became President of Sigma Chi fraternity. Upon graduation in 1970, Tom left for Officer Training School and pilot training and Patricia returned to New Jersey to teach. During Christmas of 1970, Tom went to New Jersey and proposed. They were married in November 1971.

172

VISITING HOME

General McKee always considered Cape Girardeau his hometown. He graduated from Cape Central High School in 1934 and attended Southeast Missouri State College for three years before moving on to Oklahoma University. He looked forward to his many trips back to visit family, friends, university homecomings, and especially football games when his grandson played. His youngest son, Tom, graduated from Southeast in 1970 and General McKee returned a year later to receive the university's Distinguished Service Award. He also gave the commencement address to the Class of 1971. Three of the general's grandchildren also graduated from Southeast.

His visits to Cape were always highlights for his entire family, especially for his nieces and nephews. He was a hero to them. They would constantly pester him about UFOs. He finally replied emphatically, "There is nothing in the sky that cannot be identified. There is no such thing as UFOs!"

Every night there were large family gatherings, as many as 40 to 50 attending. They never missed a chance to be in the presence of their general. The meals moved from house to house; fried fish at McKee's youngest brother Al and Peggy's, and beef roast with all the trimmings at his brother Pat and Jodi's. During those visits he was always drawn to the old homeplace and back to the farms at Whitewater and Gordonville. The last night of his visits, Seth and Sally would treat everyone to Chinese food at his favorite Cape Girardeau restaurant, Pagoda Gardens.

He was "larger than life," his sister-in-law Jodi said. "He didn't seem to us a four-star general, he was just family even though we knew he was extraordinary. He always made us feel special. It was not unusual to see him crawling around on the floor playing with the small children. Once, he gave me a supreme compliment when he announced, 'I've dined with kings and heads of state but I've never had a meal that tops this.' Seth was always honorable, dependable, and protective of us just like he was of his country." His brother Al's widow Peggy remembered, "The first time I saw Seth McKee was at Scott Air Force Base in Belleville, Illinois. When he came down the stairway of the plane dressed in full uniform, I thought he was the most handsome man I had ever seen."

Niece Tami Holshouser said, "We all idolized him. He was so sweet to us on his visits. Once, I began repeating the Gettysburg Address I had memorized in high school. Very quickly, he joined and finished with me." Nephew Brad McKee said his uncle had 98 productive years. "It was just in the last few months when he began to slip," Brad said. "Uncle Seth never changed his values. He was always relaxed around us. He was also a perfectionist. There are stories of him plowing perfect rows (straight furrows) with a team of mules in his youth."

Another niece, Missy Gum, agreed that he was larger than life. "We were enamored with his close personal relationships with military heroes such as Lt. Col. Jimmy Doolittle. At Rancho Mirage and the Thunderbird Country Club some of their friends were celebrities like Lucille Ball, Perry Como, Jonathan

Winters, Frank Sinatra, Dean Martin and Red Skelton, according to Missy. "They were especially close to Bing Crosby and the McGuire sisters. John Wayne gave him his personal gold Rolex watch, which Uncle Seth proudly wore all the time," she continued. For an invitation to one of Carol Channing's parties, she told the general, "Be sure and wear your costume," referring to his uniform.

His family said they couldn't wait for his visits. "He treated us with respect and expected us to reciprocate," nephew Jason McKee said. "Seth's favorite drink was Chivas Regal and water. He would take all of us over across the river in East Cape Girardeau, Illinois, to the Purple Crackle nightclub for more Chinese food and dancing." The family said he was a good poker player. Once, in a poker game in Las Vegas, he stared down Clint Eastwood in a sizable pot. As he raked the chips toward him he remarked to Eastwood, "I bet *that* made your day!"

Sally and the general were great hosts and especially close to Tennessee Ernie Ford. Some family members remembered the story that almost every time he was invited to the McKee's home Sally always made him sing "Sixteen Tons" before she would serve him dinner.

On one occasion, young niece Cheri McKee spent three weeks with the general and Sally in Colorado. "They treated me like a queen. I had my own room. He introduced me to Sergeant Motley who Uncle Seth told me would be my friend and take care of me during my stay. I attended all their activities and black-tie parties. At one with 16 military guests, I had Cherries Jubilee for the first time. The next morning Sergeant Motley came to my room and asked me what I wanted for breakfast. He said, 'Anything you want.' After pondering a moment, I responded, 'I think I'll have Cherries Jubilee,' and I did. Upon leaving for my return to Cape, I gave Sergeant Motley a big hug and a kiss. He had truly become my friend in that short time, and I hated to leave him. I cried as I left."

McKee and his younger brother Pat were very close even though they were eight years apart in age. They visited often and in later years made a pact to visit each other between Cape and Phoenix, Arizona, at least once a year. Phone calls became weekly and sometimes daily as the general's health deteriorated. Before triple bypass surgery, he called and told Pat he and Sally were two of only five people he knew throughout his long military career that he could count on to always do the right thing.

In 2017, Pat nominated his brother to be included on the Cape Girardeau Missouri Wall of Fame along the Mississippi River in downtown Cape Girardeau. Many citizens, along with the American Legion Post 63 and the Old Town Cape, convinced the city fathers that his portrait would be an appropriate addition to the wall. That same year he took his place on the wall between Mark Twain and General Omar N. Bradley.

On Monday, 23 October Sally and her entire family, along with several hundred admirers, assembled downtown for the official ceremony. Afterward, the crowd retired to the Cape River Heritage Museum for a reception so everyone could see the exhibit of General McKee's career and personally mix with and her family to renew old friendships.

So now "Cape's General" has a lasting effigy for all to see.

SEMO Vet Corps

In 1967, returning Vietnam War veterans formed a support group called the "SEMO Vet Corps" at Southeast Missouri State College to help returning veterans attain their degree under the GI Bill. In addition, the Corps members provided help to those vets in the transition from wartime combat situations to civilian life with its complications and challenges returning from an unpopular war. At one time the Corps represented approximately 10% of the student population. The Vet Corps lasted until 1975 when the last veterans completed their "tour" at SEMO.

In 2006 the vets returned to SEMO Homecoming for

their first reunion since 1975 to celebrate lifelong friendships formed those many years ago. It was held at the Cape Girardeau VFW, with over 100 attending. Thomas M. Meyer, U.S. Navy Seabee, described the special event: "Someone recognized General McKee as he appeared at the entrance of the banquet hall and shouted, 'Attention, General McKee on deck!' Startled, we all sprang to attention and saluted in respect. General McKee was one of us. He was a Midwesterner, a SEMO student, and from a well-respected area family. We were so impressed that he took time to come by and visit with us we still talk about him at each SEMO Homecoming. All veterans have a special bond and General McKee fit right in with us. We will never forget his honor of respect shown to us that day," Meyer said.

RETIREMENT YEARS

General McKee retired at the end of September in 1973 after 37 years of military service. At the time, he was stationed at NORAD in Colorado Springs. He and Sally decided to move to Litchfield Park on the other side of Phoenix, Arizona. In subsequent years they moved to Ponte Vedra Beach, Florida, and later to Rancho Mirage, California. They split their time between Rancho Mirage and Santa Barbara, California, depending on the weather. Sally loved the Santa Barbara area, where she enjoyed the beauty and cool temperatures of the summertime. They moved to Phoenix in 2005 at the encouragement of Seth's good friend, US Senator Barry Goldwater. In 2015, they moved "across the street" to Scottsdale to the exclusive retirement community Vi at Silverstone for Seth's final years.

While he worked part time as a consultant for several companies aligned with military industries including Grumman Corporation and Wackenhut, the McKees continued their lives similar to the ones they shared in the military—*as a team*. They golfed together, went skiing together, took cruises together, went hunting and fishing together, went camping together, visited family together, volunteered together, and danced together. In recent years, when DJs asked couples of succeeding anniversaries to please be seated, they were always the last couple dancing. Amazingly, they were dancing right up to and including Seth's 98th year. In addition, by 2014, he still held the four-star rank longer than anyone in history.

Golf

The family loved golf. Many find a late afternoon round of golf therapeutic to the stresses and demands of the workday. The McKees were no different. In fact, many privately confessed that Sally was the best. She held the lowest handicap. She won many club tournaments and together she and Seth won more than a handful. Tom tells of a special tournament: "In the mid-1990s, Pop invited me to play with him in the annual three-day, member-guest 'Out of This World' tournament at the Thunderbird Country Club in Rancho Mirage," Tom said. "On day one, we defeated Joe Coors Sr. and Jr. While very competitive, they were gracious in defeat. I knew Joe Jr. several years before when we invited him to be chairman of the Air Force Memorial.

"The final day matched us evenly in the 'alternate shot' format. On the final hole, Pop hit his approach shot within six feet of the cup. Mom recently reminded me that one of our opponents approached me and said, 'Your father has been calling you son all day…Well son, you better make this putt!' With knees knocking, I made the birdie putt and we won the championship. That evening Pop and I both received Waterford Crystal trophies, a once-in-a-lifetime event I'll never forget," Tom remembered.

Artifacts

During retirement McKee accumulated many artifacts of his service. A Red Phone is especially cherished by his family. This of course would alert presidents of impending disaster.

Another was a Rolex watch presented to him by his close friend, actor John Wayne, which he wore constantly. Yet another, a mounted jackalope, was presented by then Arizona Governor Jack Williams. His many awards would fill a fairly large museum. He was inducted into the Arizona Military Aviation Walk of Honor in 2013.

Sally Remembers

"We were very happy in our retirement years," Sally said. "Seth adjusted in stride. As we left our command, there were no aides there, so he simply picked up our luggage and we drove away.

"It gave us more time with family and especially our grandchildren and great-grandchildren. As I reflect, there were a few scary times during the war, like the time I received a telegram. Not a good sign. But thank goodness it announced Seth's promotion to colonel and commander of the 370th. Another scary time was when we were at a fishing camp up in Minnesota with the whole family, including Seth's mother and father. Seth's father took the three boys, who were very young at the time, blackberry hunting. I was afraid they might encounter a bear, and with one old man and three small boys it could have been terrible.

"My happiest moment, although there were many," Sally said, "was when I pinned Seth's first star on his uniform, with the boys looking up at him. They continued through the years—even today. When certain problems arise, they occasionally ask, 'What do you think Pop would do?'

"The night he received his first star, it was late when we went to bed. A bit later, we were surprised when the doorbell rang. I quickly opened the door and his entire staff was there to wish him congratulations. I startled them when I announced, 'Oh my gosh, you all caught me sleeping with the general!'

"Our last couple of years were at the retirement center

Vi at Silverstone in Scottsdale, Arizona," Sally said. "We were very fortunate. It is a very lovely place. When we first arrived, the residents didn't quite know how to address Seth. When they asked what they should call him, Seth simply answered, 'Well, my friends call me Seth.' They loved him from the beginning.

"Today things are a bit different with the virus. We are pretty well shut down—no congregate gatherings, food delivered to our rooms, no library, and only two at a time in elevators. Most troubling for men is the bar is closed, and for women, no beauty shop! But no virus!"

"POP"

It was a chilly, overcast morning on 13 October 2017, not the best for flight. Family and friends gathered in front of the Old Post Chapel at Fort Myer, Virginia, near Arlington National Cemetery, to pay tribute to General Seth Jefferson McKee, the highest ranking survivor of D-Day and upon reaching the age of 100, the oldest four-star general in America. The clip-clop of the horses pulling the caisson signaled the finality of the day. The assembled crowd filed slowly into the chapel to the strains of "On Eagle's Wings."

As everyone took their places in the pews, four-star General Lori Robinson, the first female four-star general in the history of the United States Armed Forces to command a major unified combatant command, took her place of honor in the front pew across the aisle from the family. Her presence representing the Air Force was especially fitting because she was the current commander of North American Aerospace Defense Command and USNORTHCOM. General McKee was CinC NORAD over 40 years earlier.

McKee's three sons, all former military pilots, gave short, eloquent eulogies of their "Pop." Tom remembered his dad saying his own mother always required the kids to attend Sunday school on a regular basis at the small country church near their farm on Whitewater Creek. "It was during this time 'Jesus Loves Me' and 'In the Garden' became Pop's favorite songs," Tom recalled. "And he sang or hummed *In the Garden* on many stressful occasions throughout his life." Tom also informed the congregation, "Pop used tough love on all three of us. He always exuded honor, respect and accountability and he expected us to follow his lead . . . and we did."

At the conclusion of the service, the congregation was escorted out of the chapel to the strains of the "Air Force Hymn." An Air Force Honor Guard squadron silently followed the caisson through the beauty and solemnity of Arlington National Cemetery's manicured fields of marble memorials to the grave site. McKee had several choices for his final resting place of honor in the hallowed grounds, but he and his family decided on a hillside among others who had fallen, in virtual shadow of the Air Force Memorial that son Tom was so instrumental in guiding to its fruition.

During the committal service, Air Force Chaplain Scott Foust uncharacteristically reviewed some of the general's accomplishments and commands, so the young men who were folding the flag would understand who they were honoring that morning. As "Taps" echoed through the hills, the roar of engines was heard through the dense fog of a "Missing Man" flyover by four A-10Cs from the 104th Fighter Squadron, Maryland Air National Guard during their appropriate tribute.

When people slowly began to disperse, the chilling sounds of a bagpipe rendition of "Danny Boy" seemed an appropriate validation of the life of one of America's greatest patriots, General Seth J. McKee, United States Air Force.

Recently the McKee men are having trouble keeping a nickel at Seth's tombstone in Arlington National Cemetery. According to Jeff, "Friday nights are traditionally a night out for old fighter pilots . . . time to ease tensions, lift one with the boys." Part of a song they sing goes:

Oh, Halleluia, Halleluia
Throw a nickel on the grass–Save a fighter pilot's ass.
Oh, Halleluia, Oh, Halleluia
Throw a nickel on the grass and you'll be saved.

So, if you ever come across the general's grave, look closely. If you can't find a nickel, do the boys a favor and leave one behind for good luck!

TRIBUTES TO
SALLY PARSHALL MCKEE

The Right Stuff

Sarah Helen Parshall, Sally McKee the Florida beauty queen. She is the first person on this earth that I loved. Yes, she is our wonderful mother, the same person that my brothers loved at first sight, the lady my father loved with all his heart.

She started her married life at 16 after being tutored and skipping a year of school. My father attended her graduation. Who would have known this young girl would be so many things to so many people? First and foremost, she was a wife and mother—always being supportive and loving to our father and constantly seeing to her boys' welfare and safety. It was not easy for a young mother whose husband was called off to war and often sent on temporary duty to foreign places. She had to perform both parental duties. She had to move often, living in 37 different homes. And that is just what they were, homes. No matter what type of quarters we had at every duty station, Mom would turn them into a home. She would then check us into schools, get us new doctors and dentists, register us in sports and hobbies, get us dancing lessons and music lessons, all the while carrying out the duties of the commander's wife at the Officer's Wives' Club, being a "Den Mother" and entertaining kings, presidents, celebrities and other dignitaries. One has to wonder where she found the time to become an excellent golfer with 11 hole-in-one trophies and numerous tournament wins to her name.

All that met her were taken by her. On one occasion, when Pop was attending a Native American ceremony, they honored him with the title of "Chief Thunder Arrow," but Mom they named "Princess Stole Our Hearts." Mom was comfortable in any setting from formal to casual. She was as much at home in the White House as she was camping, hunting, or fishing. To this very day she continues to be our example with her wisdom, strength, sensitivity, understanding, forgiveness, and love. She has what the astronauts call "the right stuff."

-Jeff McKee

The Critical Second Engine

Some lives are propelled through life by a single engine. Some lives are propelled by multi-engines. Pop preferred twin engines. He preferred the P-38 over the P-51. That preference came from the many times in WWII he was able to complete the mission and bring the aircraft safely home on one engine.

Seth and Sally launched their flight on June 7, 1941. Their union was a perfect design of mutual support— from the two engines in front to the twin booms behind. They were a beautiful couple. Their flight through life has taken them places they could not have imagined. Geographically, it covered much of the United States, Europe, and the Far East. They went higher and faster than many thought possible.

They soared, they climbed. They twisted. They turned. All in the ecstasy of the moment. It was the synchronized twin engines that made it happen.

Their missions grew in importance. They fought in WWII. They grew with the new Air Force. They represented the country internationally. They looked out into space to protect the North American continent. And through it all, they built a family. A reflection of their twin-engine design.

As they turned their airplane toward home, their now extended family became their focus. They still enjoyed putting the airplane through its paces—dancing, golfing, travelling, and visiting grandchildren.

Pop's engine began to sputter first. Mom advanced the throttle on her engine to care for him. Still, they went on to host a 100th birthday party and celebrate 75 years of marriage. That same year, Pop's engine stopped. Mom has continued on, keeping his legacy flying. And when the mission is complete, the airplane, still intact, will be brought in for a graceful landing by the critical second engine.

-Bill McKee

The Family Foundation

When Pop was born in 1916, his mother provided their family with a strong foundation of love, understanding, support, and encouragement . . . mothers do that!

A family is only as good as its foundation, much like a house, building, or even memorial. When six of us from the Air Force Association started the Air Force Memorial in 1990, we had to locate the perfect venue with a strong foundation. Where the United States Air Force Memorial stands today is just that. And it's close to Pop's final resting place.

From a personal standpoint, as a founding trustee, I was able to establish a memorial in perpetuity that would honor the concurrent Air Force service of my father and mother, as well as my two brothers and me. The symbolism of the star in the middle of the three towering spires represents, in my mind, the fact that my father obtained the rank of four-star general and had

187

three sons who served at the same time as pilots. All three of us can relate to the three spires "flying a bomb burst" around the "star."

On June 7, 1941, Pop married Sarah Helen Parshall, who was better known as Sally. He knew he was fortunate to marry the "love of his life," and Mom knew, at an early age, that Seth Jefferson McKee was going to be her partner for life. With his military assignments calling him away, it was apparent that Mom would provide the "family foundation" that was so important through WWII and all the challenges in life thereafter.

Through that strong foundation, Mom and Pop raised three boys who followed their morals, ideals, and love of family. The 75 years of marriage between them only strengthened that strong foundation for all of us.

Although Pop's service in the Army Air Corps and United States Air Force often placed him in leadership positions, he confessed that he enjoyed being in command and usually was . . . except at home! He knew the "family foundation" was because of his Sally.

Pop lived for over a century and was known and appreciated all over the world, but that would never have been possible if it wasn't for Mom. She, too, was well known and appreciated all over the world. They were a team with a strong foundation.

When Pop went to Heaven in 2016 "and touched the face of God," Mom continued to be the foundation of our family. Her love, understanding, support, and encouragement prevailed due to her inner strength. She continues to be our rock, and Pop looks down on her every day and says, "that's My Gal Sal."

-Tom McKee

APPENDIX

UNITED STATES MARINE CORPS
HEADQUARTERS, FLEET MARINE FORCE, PACIFIC
FPO, SAN FRANCISCO, 96602

In the name of the President of the United States, the Commanding General, Fleet Marine Force, Pacific takes pleasure in presenting the BRONZE STAR MEDAL to

FIRST LIEUTENANT SETH JEFFERSON MCKEE, JR.

UNITED STATES MARINE CORPS RESERVE

for service as set forth in the following

CITATION:

"For heroic achievement in connection with operations against insurgent communist (Viet Cong) forces while serving as a Forward Air Controller with Company K, Third Battalion, Ninth Marines near An Hoa, southwest of DaNang, Republic of Vietnam on 5 September 1966. During a search and clear operation, the Company was taken under heavy fire from a Viet Cong force estimated at battalion strength. Courageously and unhesitatingly exposing himself to the intense automatic weapons fire and hand grenades, First Lieutenant MCKEE personally directed air strikes upon the enemy. From his forward position, he called in the badly needed strikes and adjusted their ordnance and napalm where it was most effective. By his professional competence and exhibition of uncommon courage, First Lieutenant MCKEE helped instill the Marines with new confidence, and they moved forward to inflict heavy casualties on the enemy force. That evening, having knowledge of the terrain to his front, he volunteered to act as point for a platoon sized relief force whose mission was to break through the enemy positions, reorganize an isolated unit of Marines, and return to friendly lines. First Lieutenant MCKEE, again disregarding his own safety, led the relief force through heavy automatic weapons fire, over rugged terrain, effected the relief, and returned to friendly lines with all wounded and dead, and all the weapons the patrol could carry. Immediately on his return, he directed the medical evacuation helicopters into a small, almost inaccessible landing zone, and simultaneously directed the armed gunships in their attacks on areas where harassing fire was originating, thus keeping the landing zone open for the removal of casualties. First Lieutenant MCKEE's courage, exemplary leadership and inspiring devotion to duty were in keeping with the highest traditions of the United States Naval Service."

First Lieutenant MCKEE is authorized to wear the Combat "V".

FOR THE PRESIDENT,

V. H. KRULAK
LIEUTENANT GENERAL, U. S. MARINE CORPS
COMMANDING

TEMPORARY CITATION

Gen. McKee's Son Wins Bronze Star

DA NANG, Vietnam (ISO Marine 1st Lt. Seth J. McKee Jr., the 24-year-old son of the lieutenant general who commands U.S. Forces Japan and Fifth Air Force, has been awarded a Bronze Star for bravery under fire.

The younger McKee, a forward air controller, was decorated for personally directing air strikes from an advanced position last Sept. 5.

That same night, McKee. of Omaha, Neb., volunteered as point man for a platoon-sized relief force that broke through enemy positions, reorganized an isolated Marine unit and evacuated dead and wounded.

In the name of the President of the United States, the Commanding General, Fleet Marine Force, Pacific takes pleasure in presenting the DISTINGUISHED FLYING CROSS to

FIRST LIEUTENANT SETH JEFFERSON MCKEE, JR.

UNITED STATES MARINE CORPS RESERVE

for service as set forth in the following

CITATION:

"For heroism and extraordinary achievement in aerial flight while serving with Marine All Weather Fighter Squadron 235, Marine Aircraft Group 11, in action against insurgent communist (Viet Cong) forces in the Republic of Vietnam. On 10 March 1966, First Lieutenant MCKEE displayed keen aeronautical skill and fortitude while flying as Wingman in a two aircraft section in daring attacks against enemy positions in the As Hau Valley, where the Special Forces Camp was in imminent danger of being overrun. Fearlessly accompanying his flight leader through the steadily deteriorating weather conditions, First Lieutenant MCKEE penetrated the heavy overcast through a break, north of the target, and proceeded at extremely low altitude along a valley approach between steep mountains. Although conditions made his aircraft vulnerable to fragmentation damage from his own ordnance, he courageously delivered eight 260 pound fragmentation bombs at high speed, then pulled up sharply into the overcast to avoid the mountains. Returning again to the break in the overcast, First Lieutenant MCKEE and his flight leader again sped along the valley floor, undaunted by the danger from the automatic weapons sites, and strafed hostile positions. The daring action was of significant assistance to the defensive efforts of United States and allied forces in the beleaguered camp, forestalling an impending attack and providing time for withdrawal from the camp. First Lieutenant MCKEE's outstanding skill as an aviator, intrepid fighting spirit and unfaltering dedication to duty throughout were in keeping with the highest traditions of the United States Naval Service."

FOR THE PRESIDENT,

V. H. KRULAK
LIEUTENANT GENERAL, U. S. MARINE CORPS
COMMANDING

TEMPORARY CITATION

192

UNITED STATES AIR FORCE

THIS IS TO CERTIFY THAT

THE EXCEPTIONAL SERVICE AWARD

HAS BEEN AWARDED TO

THOMAS J. MCKEE

FOR

EXCEPTIONAL SERVICE

GIVEN UNDER MY HAND IN THE CITY OF WASHINGTON

SEPTEMBER 1998 TO SEPTEMBER 2000

SECRETARY OF THE AIR FORCE

193

CITATION TO ACCOMPANY THE AWARD OF

THE EXCEPTIONAL SERVICE AWARD

TO

THOMAS J. MCKEE

Thomas J. McKee distinguished himself in the performance of outstanding civilian service to the United States Air Force as the national president of the Air Force Association from September 1998 to September 2000. During this period, Mr. McKee contributed significantly to America's airpower awareness by informing the public of the Air Force's roles and missions in the defense of our nation. Following the first step in his AFA theme of "Congress, Industry, Grassroots," he greatly increased the AFA's presence on Capitol Hill. Working with the Air Force Office of Legislative Liaison, he led AFA's educational efforts of House and Senate members, especially first-term Congressmen. Through personal contact and at Capitol Hill receptions, Thomas McKee promoted important aerospace issues such as force modernization, recruiting and retention, and the airborne laser. His leadership enabled local AFA chapters to facilitate visits by Congressional representatives to local bases. He continued to expand his friendships with important aerospace industry leaders, always making it a point to seek their suggestions and gauge their interest in the Air Force. Mr. McKee committed his time to address the needs of all members of the Air Force community from cadets to retirees, and from active duty and reserve forces to civilian employees. He visited bases worldwide to encourage AFA activity, organization and commitment, and to show support for Air Force people and their dependents. Not only during his term as AFA president, but throughout his career, he has shown outstanding dedication and commitment to the Air Force and its people. The United States Air Force proudly bestows the Exceptional Service Award to Thomas J. McKee for his selfless service and significant contributions to the United States Air Force.

194

The Secretary of the Navy takes pleasure in presenting the
MERITORIOUS UNIT COMMENDATION to RM3 Christine D. VALENTINE, U. S. Navy

NAVAL COMMUNICATION STATION SAN DIEGO, CALIFORNIA

for service as set forth in the following

CITATION:

For meritorious service from 1 July 1967 to 31 May 1969 in direct
support of several commands, agencies, and special projects. During this
period, Naval Communication Station San Diego provided consistently outstanding service in support of two Presidential visits, the repatriation of
USS PUEBLO's crew, the Secretary of Defense consolidation policy, and
numerous tasks requiring exceptional communication and cryptologic support. Foremost among the station's exemplary accomplishments were the
planning for and execution of communications and cryptologic support for
the repatriation of PUEBLO's crew. Without precedent for guidance, handicapped by security restrictions, and tasked with its regularly-assigned
duties and responsibilities, Naval Communication Station San Diego suc-
cessfully accomplished this mission, displaying astute foresight and accuracy of planning and preparation during all phases of the operation from
its inception to conclusion ten months later. The outstanding performance
and dedication to duty demonstrated by the officers and men of Naval Communication Station San Diego, despite minimal augmentation of personnel
and with no increase in station funds, were a tribute to their profession-
alism, and were in keeping with the highest traditions of the United States
Naval Service.

All personnel attached to and serving with Naval Communication Station San Diego,
California, during the above-designated period, or any part thereof, are hereby authorized to wear the Meritorious Unit Commendation Ribbon.

For the Secretary,

T. H. Moorer

T. H. Moorer
Admiral, United States Navy
Chief of Naval Operations

Fuller Theological Seminary

SCHOOL OF THEOLOGY

The faculty and trustees have conferred upon

WILLIAM BLANCHARD MCKEE

the degree of

Master of Arts in Theology

with all the rights and privileges thereto pertaining.

Given at
Pasadena, California
on this twenty-first day of March, two thousand and fifteen

CHAIR OF THE BOARD OF TRUSTEES

DEAN OF THE SCHOOL OF THEOLOGY

PRESIDENT OF THE SEMINARY

PROVOST OF THE SEMINARY

The Sigma Chi International Fraternity

Proudly presents the honor of

Significant Sig

to

Thomas J. McKee

Epsilon Phi – Southeast Missouri State University 1970

McKee was most recently a vice president at the electronic component manufacturer Natel Engineering Co. Inc. in Chatsworth, California, serving in that role from 2010 to 2014. He retired in 2010 as a corporate director from the Northrop Grumman Corp. in Falls Church, Virginia, after 33 years in numerous positions. Earlier, McKee was commissioned in the Air Force, where he was an instructor and pilot at bases in Arizona and South Carolina. He is a former chairman and national president of the Air Force Association.

GRAND CONSUL

EXECUTIVE DIRECTOR

SOUTHEAST MISSOURI
STATE UNIVERSITY · 1873

A Resolution

by the Board of Regents
of
Southeast Missouri State University

WHEREAS, General Seth Jefferson McKee, the oldest-living American four-star general, was awarded the rank of Chevalier (Knight) in the National Order of the Legion of Honor by the government of France on Friday, November 4, 2016, the highest honor France bestows on its citizens or foreign nationals; and celebrated his 100th birthday on Saturday, November 5, 2016, at his home in Scottsdale, Arizona; and

WHEREAS, General McKee graduated from Cape Girardeau High School and attended Southeast Missouri State Teachers College from 1934 to 1937; joined the Missouri National Guard in 1935, and began his Air Force career as an aviation cadet in 1938; and completed his bachelor of arts degree in government at the University of Oklahoma in 1947; and

WHEREAS, General McKee's military career is exemplary, including serving as an airman in World War II, deployed to England in 1944 as deputy commander of the 370th fighter group, flying a Lockheed P-38 Lightning, logging more than 190 hours in 69 combat missions; he is credited with the downing of two enemy aircraft and flew cover for the D-Day invasion and was involved in bombing missions at Saint-Lo, the Falaise Gap, and Battle of the Bulge; he served in France, Belgium, and Germany; and

WHEREAS, he held positions of increasing responsibility achieving the rank of four-star general, with multiple assignments in countries throughout the world, and he retired in 1973 as commander of the North American Air Defense Command; and

WHEREAS, his military honors and awards include the Air Force Distinguished Service Medal, Silver Star, Legion of Merit with two oak leaf clusters, Distinguished Flying Cross, Air Medal with 10 oak leaf clusters, Croix de Guerre with Palm (France), Croix de Guerre with Palm (Belgium), Belgian Fourragere, Order of Leopold with Palm (Belgium), First Class Order of the Crown of Thailand, Order of the Sacred Treasure, First Class (Japan), and Order of National Security Merit, Second Class (Republic of Korea); and

WHEREAS, General McKee has been married to his lovely wife, Sally, for more than 75 years, and the P-38 he flew was named in her honor as "My Gal Sal," and they raised three sons, Seth, William and Thomas, and Sally played an important role and worked in hospitals as a "Gray Lady," an American Red Cross volunteer; and

WHEREAS, General McKee has represented the University well during his career and has supported his alma mater by presenting the commencement address in May 1971, and by returning to campus often to speak with faculty, staff, and students; he received the Missouri Mule Skinner citation and the Alumni Merit Award from Southeast, both in 1971; and he has been faithful in his stewardship of the public trust,

Now, therefore, be it resolved by the Board of Regents of Southeast Missouri State University that sincere congratulations and the grateful appreciation of the University community be expressed to General Seth Jefferson McKee, and that this resolution be placed in the minutes of the Board of Regents;

Done in the City of Cape Girardeau, Missouri, this sixteenth day of December in the year two thousand sixteen.

President of the Board of Regents

President of the University

ATTEST:

Secretary

198

Proclamation

Whereas, before his death at 100 years of age, General Seth McKee was our Nation's highest-ranking D-Day survivor, who earned four stars while serving under six Presidents in the Air Force, and retiring from his post as the Commander of North American Aerospace; and

Whereas, McKee was a 1934 graduate of Cape Girardeau High School and attended Southeast Missouri State Teachers College; and

Whereas, McKee has been universally honored at home and abroad, being called a "guardian angel" to the Allied Forces and having been bestowed, in November 2016, France's rank of Chevalier in the National Order of the Legion of Honor; and

Whereas, his tremendous bravery powered him through successful battles and missions, that he had no fear of death, while preserving an unabashed respect for life; and

Whereas, he remained humble and family-focused throughout a lengthy and successful career, reportedly declining awards and ceremonies save for the opportunities to allow his grandchildren to witness history; and

Now, Therefore, Be It Resolved that I, Harry Rediger, Mayor of the City of Cape Girardeau, Missouri, do hereby recognize, for his courage and character,

General Seth McKee

In Witness Whereof I have hereunto set my hand and caused to be affixed the Seal of the City of Cape Girardeau, Missouri, this 9th day of **January, 2017.**

_____
Harry E. Rediger, Mayor

199

McKee Family	General and Mrs. Seth Jefferson McKee
Seth J. McKee, Jr. USMC '63 – '68 William B. McKee USAFA '68 Thomas J. McKee SEMO '70	Lt Col – USAF Vietnam – USMC Capt – USAF Vietnam Era Capt – USAF Vietnam Era

McKee Recognition in Southeast Missouri State University's
Veterans Plaza

· THREE SPIRES ·

Majestic sentinels curving toward the blue
Standing guard o'er the fallen
Arching sunward through the dew

High on a bluff, inspiration to all
With an aerial salute
To answer the call

Three spires of steel,
Freedom's wings of might,
Surrounding a star
Forever in flight

By Jerry Ford
In Memory

HIGH FLIGHT

Oh! I have slipped the surly bonds of Earth
And danced the skies on laughter-silvered wings

Sunward I've climbed, and joined the tumbling mirth
Of sun-split clouds, and done a hundred things
You have not dreamed of – wheeled and soared and swung
High in the sunlit silence. Hov'ring there,
I've chased the shouting wind along and flung
My eager craft through footless halls of air

Up, up the long, delirious burning blue
I've topped the wind-swept heights with easy grace
Where never lark, or ever eagle flew-
And, while with silent, lifting mind I've trod
The high untresspassed sanctity of space,
Put out my hand, and touched the face of God.

~ John Gillespie Magee, Jr.

Index

Symbols

1st Pursuit Squadron   89
3rd Battalion 9th Marines   164
36th Fighter Bomber Group   xviii
104th Fighter Squadron   183

A

Air Force Academy   105, 165, 167
Air Force Association   167–168, 187
Air Force Memorial   137, 167–168, 179, 183, 187
Air Force Memorial Foundation   167–168
Allied Expeditionary Forces   147
Alpha Chi Omega sorority   172
American Airlines   164
Apollo 8   171
Arc de Triomphe   152
Arlington National Cemetery   168, 182–184
Army Air Corps   53, 82, 84–85, 91, 146, 188

B

Baton Rouge   75
Battle of the Bulge   92, 114
Bloomberg, Red   29–30
Box Supper   28
Bradley, Omar   176
Brisbane, Australia   96
Broadmoor Hotel   18
Bush, Geo. W   168

C

Café Rouge   161
California Air National Guard   164
Cape River Heritage Museum   176
Central High School, Cape Girardeau   36–38, 173
Centrifugal Force   45
Chandelles   95
Cheyenne, Wyoming   70, 119, 120, 143, 171
Chief Thunder Arrow   186
Chivas Regal   175

Chung-hee, Park   103
CinC NORAD   182
Ciphering   17
Citadel, South Carolina   161
Civil War   4, 11, 24
Colorado Springs, Colorado   18, 70, 143–144, 167, 178
Combat Fox   104
Commander US Forces and 5th Air Force   xviii
Cotton Belt Railroad   3
Cousin, Vincent   154
Crawford, Ollie   168
Creighton University, Nebraska   163
Cuban Eights   95

D

Damewood, Lawrence   95
Da Nang, Vietnam   164
D-Day   xviii, xix, 91, 112, 147, 155, 182
Democratic National Convention   103
Desert Storm   152, 153
Distinguished Service Award   173
Douglas, George   168
Dun & Bradstreet   62

E

Eglin Field, Florida   89
Eisenhower, Dwight   128, 147
Ellsworth Air Force Base, South Dakota   xviii, 165
Ent Air Force Base, Colorado   xviii
Experimental Aircraft Association   164

F

Falcon Service Club   162
Fifth Air Force   100
Florida State University   161
"Fork-tailed devils"   91
Fort Sill, Oklahoma   83–84
Frisco Railroad   3
Fuchu Air Station, Japan   xviii
Fuller Seminary, Pasadena, California   166

G

Gallagher, Coach   73–76

Gettysburg Address   174
"Gray Lady"   161
Great Depression   76, 149
Great Salt Lake   66
Grumman Aerospace Corporation   167
"Guardian Angels"   91

H

Habitat for Humanity   164
Hand-hewn Logs   24
Hart, C. Munroe   105
Headquarters Co., 140th Infantry   51
"Hellzapoppin"   161
"High Flight"   202
Hirohito, Emperor   151
Homestead AFB, 823rd Air Division Florida Commander   xviii
"Honky-Tonks"   72
Hotel Pennsylvania   161
Hunter AFB, Georgia 2nd Bombardment Wing Deputy Commander
    xviii

I

Immelmann   95
'In the Garden'   11, 183
Italian Air Force Rome, Italy   xviii

J

"Jesus Loves Me"   11
Johnson, Lyndon   130, 147

K

Kennedy, John   147
Kennedy, Robert   103
King, Martin Luther, Jr   103
Kingsville, Texas   164
Korean Conflict   97

L

Lackland Air Force Base, Texas   167
"Lanes in the Road"   105
Laughlin Air Force Base, Texas   165
Little Bambino   170
Little Chiefs of Staff   151

LSU   75

M

March Air Force Base, California, 12th Air Force   xviii
Marine Air Group 2   164
Marine Aviation Cadet (MarCad)   163
Marine Corps   163, 164, 171–172
Maryland Air National Guard   183
McGehee, Arkansas   xvii, 2–3
McKee, Al and Peggy   174
McKee Award   133, 157
McKee, Bill   136, 187
McKee, Jeff   xv, 90, 93, 133–134, 136, 162–163
McKee, "Neit"   2–3, 6, 13, 27, 35, 37, 42, 49, 109
McKee, Pete   13, 18–19, 25, 40, 71, 109
McKee, Sally   xv, 27, 89, 96, 126, 133–134, 150–151, 160–162, 166, 169–188
McKee, Tom   xv, 131, 133–135, 138, 162, 166–168, 170–171, 172–173, 179,
    183, 188
McKee, Wm F (Pat)   3, 109, 121, 174, 176
Memorial Foundation (USAF)   167–168
MENSA   164
Military Code of Conflict (US)   105
Miller, Glenn   161
Misawa, Japan   97, 99
Miss Florida Citrus   27, 134, 160
Missing Man Formation   183
Miss New Jersey   172
Missouri National Guard   44, 51, 88
Missouri Wall of Fame   138, 176
Model T Ford   16
Molasses   23, 24
Montgomery, Alabama   166
Moorer, Thomas H.   106
Motley, Sgt.   175
Myrtle Beach Air Force Base, South Carolina   167

N

Nagoya, Japan   97
National Guard, 140th Infantry
    51
Niigata, Japan   97
Nixon, Richard   119, 131, 143–144, 148
NORAD   xvii–xix, 30, 95, 117, 143–145, 148, 153, 178, 182
Normal School, Cape Girardeau   43

North Korea   104–105
North Pole   152

O

Officer's Wives' Club   186
Offutt Air Force Base, Nebraska   xviii
"O Hallelujah, Hallelujah"   184
Oklahoma State (A&M)   73, 75
Oklahoma University   77, 85, 173
Old Orlando Air Base   160
Old Post Chapel   182
Old Town Cape   176
Omaha Beach   91
Omaha, Nebraska   162, 166
"On Eagle's Wings"   182
Osan Air Base   104
Oswald, Lee Harvey   147
Ozark National Scenic Riverways   171

P

Pagoda Gardens   174
Paradise Valley, Arizona   166
Patriot Missiles   153
Pattillo, Charles Curtis "Buck"   95–96
Pattillo, Cuthbert A. "Bill"   95–96
Power Squadron   171
Pueblo, USS   xix, 103–106
Purple Crackle Club   175

R

Raider   169, 170
Rancho Mirage   174, 178–179
Randolph Air Force Base, Texas   165
Reese Air Force Base, Texas   167
Robinson, Coach   39
Roosevelt, Franklin   127, 144, 146

S

Scott Air Force Base, Belleville, Illinois   174
Semi-Automatic Ground Environment (SAGE) radar   144
Seoul, South Korea   104
Shea, Martha   45
Shooting Stars   95

Sigma Chi Fraternity   167
"Sixteen Tons"   175
Skyblazers   116
Southeast Missouri State University   ii, xiv, xiv–xv, xix, 43, 166, 200
Strategic Air Command   xviii

T

Tet Offensive   103
The Right Stuff   185–186
"Three Spires"   201
Thunderbird Country Club   174, 179
Tokyo, Japan   89, 96, 100–101
Truman, Harry   127, 144, 147
Twain, Mark   176
Typhoon Vance   97

U

UCLA   64, 165
USNORTHCOM   182

V

Valentine, Christine   105
VE Day   115–116, 152

Y

Yokota Air Base, Japan   96